5.00

The
Japanese
Character

HASEGAWA NYOZEKAN

A JAPANESE NATIONAL COMMISSION FOR UNESCO PUBLICATION

The Japanese Character

A Cultural Profile

By NYOZEKAN HASEGAWA
translated by JOHN BESTER

Published by
KODANSHA INTERNATIONAL LTD.
Tokyo, Japan   Palo Alto, California, U.S.A.

DISTRIBUTORS:

British Commonwealth (excluding Canada and the Far East)
WARD LOCK & COMPANY LTD.
London

France
HACHETTE—LIBRAIRIE ETRANGERE
Paris

Continental Europe (excluding France)
BOXERBOOKS, INC.
Zurich

The Far East
JAPAN PUBLICATIONS TRADING COMPANY
C.P.O. Box 722, Tokyo

Published by KODANSHA INTERNATIONAL LTD., 3-19 Otowa-cho, Bunkyo-ku, Tokyo, Japan and KODANSHA INTERNATIONAL (U.S.A.) LTD., 577 College Avenue, Palo Alto, California 94306. © Ministry of Education, Japan, 1965. All rights reserved. Printed in Japan.
First edition, 1966
Library of Congress Catalog Card No.66-19819

FOREWORD OF THE JAPANESE NATIONAL COMMISSION FOR UNESCO

The General Conference of Unesco, at its ninth session held in New Delhi in 1956, decided to launch the Major Project on Mutual Appreciation of Eastern and Western Cultural Values.

In response to the decision, the Japanese National Commission for Unesco has been carrying on, since 1958, a long-term program of publishing modern Japanese philosophical works translated into foreign languages.

We have so far brought out the following five books: *The Ways of Thinking of Eastern Peoples* by Hajime Nakamura; *A Study of Good* by Kitaro Nishida; *A Climate* by Tetsuro Watsuji; *Time and Eternity* by Seiichi Hatano; and *Studies in Shinto Thought* by Tsunetsugu Muraoka. The present volume is the sixth of the series.

Mr. Nyozekan Hasegawa, author of this book, is well known not only in Japan but also abroad as one of the most eminent scholarly critics of Japanese culture and social life. It is hoped that this volume will prove useful to those foreign scholars and students who wish to get acquainted with the culture of the Japanese people and their ways of thinking.

Our acknowledgement is due to the author, Mr. Nyozekan Hasegawa, to Prof. Tetsushi Furukawa of Tokyo University and Mr. Ryuichi Kaji, former Chief Editor of the Asahi Press, who have co-operated in the compilation of this volume, and also to Mr. John Bester for the translation.

December 1965

Japanese National Commission
for Unesco

TABLE OF CONTENTS

Illustrations follow page 68

ORIGINAL PREFACE (1938)

This book gathers together some of the essays on the Japanese character and related subjects which I have published in the years since 1935. During those years, there has been much talk of the Japanese spirit and the superiority of things Japanese. Such talk can have little meaning, however, unless founded on a practical awareness among the Japanese of their own character, on which everything else depends. In fact, very little has been written on the subject, so I have concentrated here on this aspect. In writing of the "Japanese character," thus, I was less interested in showing what it ought to be than what it is. Such an approach necessarily requires a knowledge of both the national virtues and the national shortcomings. In this book, the emphasis is on the virtues; it seemed appropriate to start from them, since not only do foreigners labor under misapprehensions as to their nature but even the Japanese themselves frequently misinterpret them.

Any study of the Japanese character must have reference to Japanese history in general, as well as to particular cultural forms found in Japanese literature, art, and other similar fields. This work is, as it were, a kind of introduction to the subject, both for the reader and for the author himself. I have accordingly selected the articles of a more general nature, omitting the pieces on more specialized subjects written either earlier or around the same time.

I was originally asked to write Chapters IV and V as a kind of elementary introduction to the Japanese character for the benefit of foreigners, while some material is taken from talks originally given to audiences from entirely different walks of life.

I wish to express my gratitude to the original publishers who have given me permission to reproduce the essays in this book.

H.N.

December, 1938

PREFACE, 1965

In view of my original aims in writing the pieces in this book, which I described in my original preface, I am delighted that the Japanese National Commission for UNESCO should have decided to publish it in English translation. I would emphasize here that the views expressed in this work are entirely my own, and may well conflict with theories concerning the Japanese character expressed by earlier writers, both Japanese and foreign. I shall be all the more grateful, therefore, for any opinions and criticisms the work may call forth from my readers.

H.N.

TRANSLATOR'S NOTE

Of all the shadowy figures who are liable to intrude themselves between the reader and his book, the translator should normally have the least claim on his attention. However, an exception may perhaps be made for him when he has made over into English, more or less as it stands, a work on a comparatively abstruse subject written in a language as remote from our own as Japanese. Precisely because this is not an "adaptation" for the Western reader—because it sets out to provide a reasonably complete and accurate translation—a few notes on some of the difficulties posed by a Japanese work of this nature may be in order.

To deal with practical questions first: the essays which constitute the main body of the work known in Japanese as *Nihonteki Seikaku* have been translated with only insignificant cuts. An appendix containing a number of more or less verbatim transcriptions of talks on similar subjects given by the author on various different occasions has, with the author's permission, been omitted because it covered little new ground. However, a few passages which seemed too good to waste have been rescued and grafted into the main text. For the rest, I have tampered with the text as little as possible. "Faithful translation," of course, is sometimes made an excuse for a product in which the translator has not taken the trouble to ensure that what he has written is really meaningful (or at least what the author believed to be meaningful), which is an insult to the intelligence of both author and reader. Here, I have taken liberties with the sentence patterns and order only in the attempt to achieve true "meaningfulness" in English.

The temptation to adapt or précis is, indeed, strong. I feel—and many Japanese seem to feel the same—that modern Japanese, even today and still less over thirty years ago when this work was written, is not yet a very flexible and precise medium for speculative writing. Experience in translating all kinds of Japanese has left me with the feeling that the thinker who tries to express something too original or too abstract is faced with the task of forging his own language with which to communicate with the reader. The attempt is not always successful (I venture to say this only after having tested various such attempts at communication on my Japanese friends). Perhaps it is an awareness of this difficulty that makes some Japanese writers tend to repeat themselves, or to lead the reader along only by the very easiest stages.

Nor is the Japanese feeling for the organization of an argument always the same as ours. In some Japanese writers, particularly of the old school, a digression embarked on quite casually may lead to another, and then another, and the main argument is skittering away out of sight before the dismayed reader really realizes what is happening. Then there is the tendency of Japanese logic to effect what I can only describe as a spiralling movement. This is not the same as going round in circles. The reader does not find himself back where he started: there has been progress, though not necessarily in the direction in which he appeared to be traveling at any given moment. Nevertheless, this tendency, combined with the tendency to digress, undoubtedly gives the Western reader an occasional feeling of drifting aimlessly.

The style of *The Japanese Character* may show some features that will irritate the Western reader, but I do not feel basically that it drifts. The river of its argument may flow at a leisurely pace, it may have its whirlpools and its backwaters, but the river is still there, and the reader who lets himself be carried along on it is likely to find his outlook on the subject in hand subtly changed, whatever reserva-

tions he may have about specific conclusions or the methods by which they are reached.

Perhaps the chief value of the work lies in its nature as an attempt by a Japanese to analyze the unchanging mainsprings of the Japanese character and cultural tradition from a viewpoint which is aware of the West yet firmly placed within that tradition. As such, it offers a number of new insights and suggests a number of new angles of approach. For some readers these will help in correcting conclusions based on false analogies with Western society and ways of thought. For others, they will serve to give clearer shape to things already apprehended vaguely through direct experience of modern Japan. A second claim on the reader's attention is the work's position in the history of modern Japanese thought and society. As a study written in the difficult pre-war period, a study which still commands the respect of large numbers of thinking Japanese, its social and psychological significance is great, and the very ways in which it sets about reaching its conclusions are important for the light they throw on characteristically Japanese thought-patterns. It may be of interest, too, to apply the author's ideas to what actually happened following publication of his work—the war, for example, or the reaction of the Japanese to defeat and the problems of postwar society.

A basic minimum of notes has been provided to help the reader who has no knowledge of Japanese history or literature. Except for the cover and title page, all Japanese names are given in the Japanese style, which places the surname before the given name.

JOHN BESTER

tions he may have about specific conclusions or the methods by which they are reached.

Perhaps the chief value of the work lies in its nature as an attempt by a Japanese to analyze the unchanging mainsprings of the Japanese character and cultural tradition from a viewpoint which is aware of the West yet firmly placed within that tradition. As such, it offers a number of new insights and suggests a number of new angles of approach. For some readers these will help in correcting conclusions based on false analogies with Western societies and ways of thought. For others, they will serve to give clearer shape to things already apprehended vaguely through direct experience of modern Japan. A second claim on the reader's attention is the work's position in the history of modern Japanese thought and society. As a study written in the difficult pre-war period, a study which still commands the respect of large numbers of thinking Japanese, its social and psychological significance is great, and the very ways in which it sets about reaching its conclusions are important for the light they throw on characteristically Japanese thought-patterns. It may be of interest too, to apply the author's ideas to what actually happened following publication of his work—the war, for example, or the reaction of the Japanese to defeat and the problems of post-war society.

A basic minimum of notes has been provided to help the reader who has no knowledge of Japanese history or literature. Except for the cover and title page, all Japanese names are given in the Japanese style, which places the surname before the given name.

John Bester

HASEGAWA NYOZEKAN
THE MAN AND HIS WORK
KAJI RYŪICHI

I

Hasegawa Manjirō, better known by his pen name of Hasegawa Nyozekan, was born on November 30, 1875, the second son of a prosperous merchant family in the area of Tokyo known as *shita-machi*—the low-lying districts, close to the sea and the river Sumida, which have been known for centuries as the home of the merchants and artisans who symbolized the essential spirit of the capital. He was born one year to the day after Winston Churchill, the great British statesman. That this writer—widely accorded a place in the first rank as a thinker in the English tradition, a writer on social affairs, and a journalist—should have been born only a year after the greatest figure modern England has produced is—though in itself no more than a coincidence—an interesting fact. Both lived to be over ninety (Hasegawa is now ninety-one); both experienced directly a period of nearly one hundred years in which mankind underwent the most epochmaking changes and development in its history; and both applied their brains directly to the significance of what they had seen and heard.

When Ieyasu, the first of the Tokugawa shoguns, moved from the province of Mikawa on the Pacific side of central Honshū to Edo (now Tokyo), he brought with him five official carpenters to direct construction of the Shogun's residence. One of these was Nyozekan's direct ancestor, and his family lived in Edo from that time on. Following the Meiji Restoration, his family became timber merchants living in the Fukagawa district of Tokyo, running a business called

"Mikawa-ya" after the name of the province whence the family had sprung. The family was deeply imbued with respect for Japanese traditions, and for the traditional outlook of the artisan of old Edo, yet at the same time its prevailing atmosphere was in no way at variance with the more progressive outlook that marked the newly-arising modern industry of the early Meiji era. In short, the family maintained an enlightened, non-aristocratic outlook which accorded well with the requirements of the new age.

The family also ran a second business, of a kind not to be found anywhere else at the time. In the amusement quarter of Tokyo known as Asakusa, on the wooded hill behind the great old Buddhist temple that forms its focal point, the family owned a children's amusement park consisting of a privately-run zoo and a circus. Such a project—a kind of Coney Island or Disneyland in miniature, run by a single family—was of course unique in early Meiji Japan (it was started in 1883, when Nyozekan was eight), and the park enjoyed enormous popularity among adults from all walks of life as well as the children.

Nyozekan, thus, was brought up as a member of a family of means and culture in an atmosphere of sympathy for the traditional outlook of the artisan class; he was educated in the progressive modern ideas of the early Meiji era; and he grew up, moreover, in an atmosphere of love for all living creatures. It followed that he was equipped by birth with the most important elements required for understanding Japan and the character of its people, and for describing and ex-plaining them to readers in Japan and abroad.

2

Nyozekan was born a mere seven years after the Meiji Restoration of 1868. Education at the time was still basically classical, centering around ancient Japanese and Chinese literature, with a superimposi-

tion of modern ideas from abroad. These new, foreign ideas all derived, roughly speaking, from three principles: liberalism, democracy, and humanism. Until the middle of the Meiji era, the ideas of modern America, Britain, and France poured in in a steady stream. In time, they began to exert a great influence on every aspect of Japanese cultural, economic, and political life, Nyozekan himself being brought into particularly close contact with liberal and democratic ideas of the British type.

When he was nine, he was sent with his elder brother to a private academy run by Tsubouchi Yūzō (Tsubouchi Shōyō), the great expert on English literature who was one of the oldest and most respected professors of Waseda University, celebrated as the translator of Shakespeare's complete works. Shōyō was an acquaintance of Nyozekan's father, who ran the publishing firm which had put out his first book. From the age of ten, Nyozekan started attending the Dōjinsha English Academy run by Nakamura Masanao (pen name Nakamura Keiu). Nakamura was an English scholar and former retainer of the Shogunate who before the Restoration had been to study in England, and who achieved fame shortly after the Restoration with his Japanese translation of Smiles' *Self-Help*. Next, Nyozekan entered the Kyōritsu School in Kanda (later the Kaisei Middle School), but soon left and for a while studied at the Tokyo English School (later the Nippon Middle School) run by Sugiura, a well-known Chinese scholar who had been to England shortly after the Meiji Restoration to study agricultural chemistry at Manchester University. Sugiura later became an editorial writer for the *Asahi Shimbun,* and in late life was director of studies for the present Emperor, then Crown Prince; he was an educator of the highest caliber, combining in himself the best qualities of the Japanese samurai and the English gentleman.

Next, Nyozekan entered the Tokyo College of Legal Studies, which taught chiefly English law and was later to develop into the present Chūō University. This was at the earnest desire of his father,

who wanted him to become a lawyer. He finally graduated at the age
of twenty-three. His education had given him a chance to absorb
Oriental thought via the Japanese classics and Chinese philosophy,
while at the same time exposing him constantly to English ideas and
to a moral atmosphere that owed much to the English concept of the
gentleman. It is for this reason that Nyozekan, throughout his life,
has been known as thinker and journalist of the English school.

3

Although Nyozekan specialized in legal studies in accordance with
his father's wishes, his own ambitions lay not so much in the legal
profession as in journalism. His elder brother, in fact, had worked
first for the *Yamato Shimbun,* then for the Tokyo *Asahi Shimbun,* where
he was one of the most active members of the City Section, also
writing stories and essays in his leisure hours. Around this time, men
such as Mutsu Minoru (Ketsunan) and Miyake Yūjirō (Setsurei) were
putting out a type of newspaper known in Japanese as *ō-shimbun*
("major newspaper") which specialized in critical writing, as opposed to the *ko-shimbun* ("minor newspaper") which concentrated
on topical items of more vulgar interest. One of these newspapers
was the *Nippon Shimbun,* and it was Nyozekan's secret ambition to
become a writer on social affairs for this newspaper. Above all, he
wanted to become a "man of ideas" who, through his newspaper
work, could help form public opinion.

While he was at college, he had begun to take an interest in
criminal psychology as a kind of sideline to his legal studies, and the
first work of a serious nature which he published, at the age of
twenty-one, was a short story, "Futasujimichi," which describes
with great compassion how a working boy is led to commit a crime
out of sympathy for the plight of an older woman with whom he is
on friendly terms. The story was entered in a contest run by one

of the top magazines of the day, and won high praise from leading critics. Thus Nyozekan's life as a writer began, not in the field of criticism, but in that of creative writing.

When he was around twenty-four, Nyozekan began contributing to the *Nihon Shimbun*, thus marking the beginning of his life as a journalist. Yet at the same time he was frequenting the Imperial Library at Ueno, where he read large numbers of foreign works. In this way, he got through most of the standard works on criminal psychology, anarchism and socialism. He made translation with commentary of the autobiography of the aristocratic Russian revolutionary Kropotkin, and had it published serially in the *Nihon Shimbun*. He also contributed articles on the question of crime, and had a number of short stories on similar themes published in the *Tokyo Asahi*. At last, he had got a firm foothold in the world of journalism.

Finally, in the autumn of his twenty-eighth year, his dream came true, and he was given a post with the *Nihon Shimbun*. The president of the *Nihon,* Mutsu Ketsunan, was a student of French ideas with a special knowledge of Comte, while his collaborator Miyake Setsurei was more knowledgable in English studies, being particularly attracted by Spencer. It was through them that Nyozekan made his first acquaintance with the pragmatic philosophy of Comte and the social theories of Spencer.

The motive originally inspiring the formation of the *Nihon Shimbun* was resistance to the facile "Westernization" of the so-called Rokumeikan era—the German ideas and German Constitution imported in such haste in the mid-Meiji era by the clan oligarchy of Itō Hirobumi and his followers and by the bureaucracy, along with the sudden burst of idolatry of all things foreign which this provoked. Its professed ideals were based on an enlightened nationalism—not the rabid kind which was later to become so familiar in Japan, but a more rational insistence that it was necessary for Japan to learn, not only from the progressive ideas of the British

and French, but from their healthy conservatism as well.

The newspaper came out strongly against the Prussian-style emphasis on the granting of a constitution suddenly introduced by Itō Hirobumi and his followers, around the period from 1885 to 1890, out of fear lest excessively democratic ideas should spring up from below as a result of human rights already bestowed from above. It also opposed the way the government proposed to take the unification of the Prussian Empire as a model for its work in Japan. It expressed grave concern at the way the Meiji Constitution followed the example of the Prussian Constitution in setting the Emperor above everything, with the civil government and the military on equal terms beneath him. Such a formula, it warned, would inevitably lead in the end to the military's getting its own way and the plunging of the country into militarism and anti-democratism.

It was factors such as these that nurtured the characteristic outlook—the basic partiality for British ways of thinking and the anti-Germanism—for which Nyozekan has always been known and which he has maintained consistently to the age of ninety-one. In fact, what came to pass was just what he and his colleagues had most feared, and Japan was brought to ruin in just the same way as the Germany on which it had modeled itself.

4

The family home at Fukagawa in the *shitamachi* district, where the timber-yards stood, was an imposing affair with grounds large enough to embrace a wood and a Shinto shrine within their bounds. In later years, the alternate success and failure of Nyozekan's father's business took the family to a succession of homes in various parts of Tokyo, but the effect on Nyozekan's character of the atmosphere of culture and enlightenment which he breathed in early childhood was to stay with Nyozekan all the rest of his life. His intellectual

background, too, was extremely unusual. His elder brother Yama-moto Shōgetsu, a newspaper writer in the tradition of the humorous and satirical writers of popular novelettes in the Edo period, later became chief of the City Section of the *Tokyo Asahi,* while his younger brother was one of the most talented pupils of Mizuno Toshi-kata, last of the ukiyo-e print artists.

On top of this, as we have seen, Nyozekan lived his childhood and youth in an atmosphere of English-style—and to some extent French-style—scholarship. It is no wonder that he showed such an active, questing intellect. Even when his dream came true and he was taken on by the *Nihon Shimbun,* he still found time to carry on his studies of criminal psychology, and actually served as part-time member of the Criminal Law Research Center of Tokyo Imperial University. Hearing that the study of crime was especially advanced in Italy, he enrolled part time at the Tokyo College of Foreign Languages at Hitotsubashi in order to study Italian. On top of this, his inborn love of study led him to dabble in many other subjects, among them sociology, philosophy, theology, psychology, history, anthropology, archaeol-ogy, and folklore. All this he managed in the intervals of his busy life as a newspaperman.

At the same time, he continued his creative writing, turning out an increasing number of works in both serious and lighter veins—essays, travel writing, and poetry in addition to his novels and short stories.

With the retirement of Mutsu Minoru due to illness, the *Nihon Shimbun* which Nyozekan had so idolized and which had had such a following among the informed public of the day began to totter and eventually went bankrupt. Miyake Setsurei and a number of the more hard-headed of its members joined with Miyake's magazine *Nihonjin* (Japanese) and continued publication, under the name of "Japan and the Japanese," from a firm with which Miyake was connected. It proved impossible, however, for the magazine to support such a large number of newspapermen of the first rank, and the larger part

of them were taken over by the *Asahi Shimbun*.

When Nyozekan was thirty-one he in his turn, together with a number of his colleagues, resigned from the newspaper. Then in early 1907, when he was thirty-three, he joined the Osaka *Asahi Shimbun* and embarked on an active and varied life as a member of its staff. Most of his colleagues who knew him at that time are dead by now. According to the two or three who still survive, however, it was Nyozekan who first introduced a modern atmosphere and scientific methods of management at the Osaka *Asahi*. His work there served to raise the reputation of the newspaper and, in turn, the level of Japanese journalism as a whole. He did work for the foreign news, communications, and make-up sections, and also wrote editorials and a column on current topics, as well as publishing, in serial form, novels which he used as vehicles for his ideas, and full-length travel journals. When he was thirty-five, he was sent to England for the Anglo-Japanese Exposition, and was present at the funeral of Edward VII, with which his visit happened to coincide.

Nyozekan stayed with the Osaka *Asahi* for some ten years, playing an important part in its affairs as city editor and editorial writer. World War I came and went, and fluctuations in the postwar economic world began to create social unrest in various forms. With its outspoken criticisms of the way the country's affairs were being run, the Osaka *Asahi* gradually incurred the displeasure of the bureaucrats and military men who formed the government, and re-pressive measures became increasingly severe. Gradually, the idea became widespread among right-wing elements that the Osaka *Asahi* harbored "dangerous thoughts."

5

The Osaka *Asahi* was strongly affected by the general democratic atmosphere which had pervaded the world following World War I

and even reached Japan. Under the leadership of editor Torii Sosen and Nyozekan himself, who was city editor, it made frequent attacks on the Terauchi Government of the day. The Russian Revolution of 1919 and the revolution in Germany that occurred the following year provided a strong stimulus to left-wing and revolutionary ideas all over the world, Japan included. The situation was aggravated in Japan by a sharp rise in the price of rice and by certain unscrupulous rice merchants who, despite the unsettled state of the public temper, set out to corner the market. The Osaka *Asahi* exposed what was going on. At the same time, it opposed the sending of troops to Siberia by the Terauchi Government. In the summer of 1918, ''rice riots'' occurred and spread all over the country.

The Terauchi Government, the military, and right-wing organizations all alike viewed the *Asahi* with hostility, and determined to clamp down on it firmly as soon as the chance occurred. A pretext was found in a passage in an *Asahi* article relating to the rice riots, which allegedly violated a regulation concerning the publication of matter prejudicial to the maintenance of law and order. As a result of the incident, both Torii and Hasegawa were forced to take the responsibility and resign from their posts, and they were followed shortly after by almost all the other executive staff of the Osaka *Asahi*. This incident was matched by another known as the ''Asahi Shimbun Affair.'' From that time until the present—a full forty-seven years—Nyozekan has been a freelance writer. For more than fifteen years he himself ran two magazines—*Warera* (''Ourselves'') and *Hihan* (''Criticism'')—and at the same time he had a potent effect on public opinion via the press and radio. His writings and talks have been collected and have appeared in a number of volumes.

Nyozekan, who has always devoted a lot of time to the study of Western learning, has applied the rationalistic outlook of modern science to a throughgoing reappraisal of the classical scholarship of China and Japan. By reading, digesting, and assimilating the latter in this way, he has worked out a new, uniquely personal approach to

writing on cultural affairs, an approach which combined the outlooks of both the East and the West. So unusually wide is the range
of his interests that he has been referred to as an "encyclopedist"—
a most unusual type in Japan. With a broad, rich power of observa-
tion which is rooted in a love of mankind yet can also be biting, displaying at times an almost Shavian irony, he has developed a rare sense
of judgement of things and values, which he himself refers to as the
"philosophy of common sense." Throughout all his work, his
constant companions have been the Chinese *Book of Odes* (*Shih-ching*)
and the works of Lao-tzu, together with the two Japanese classics
Manyōshū and *Kojiki,* which he regards as indispensable to a knowledge of the freer, more natural Japan of ancient times.

6

Nyozekan's views were based from first to last on an English-style
positivism, pragmatism, and rationalism, which he sought to give
expression in his writings and lectures as a means of guiding public
opinion. The point of view he expressed was in every way progressive,
yet he avoided the violent flights of fancy which characterized
German and Russian thinkers. He preferred to blend his progressive-
ness with a respect for national tradition, and saw the need to learn,
as we have already seen, from the better aspects of English and
French conservatism. In short, he was a firm and consistent opponent
of German-style theorists who spent all their time, whether among
the governing or the governed, in pointless intellectualizing and
playing with ideologies.

Against the German-style, bureaucratic approach to government
of the day he set a modern, popular spirit, and he worked to counter
inhuman German-style militarism and aggression with democracy,
liberalism, humanism, and pacifism. The militarism and aggression
into which Japan under the control of the military and bureaucracy

seemed to be plunging at such a rapid rate from the time of the Manchurian Incident aroused his resistance and his fierce love of his country to the point where they crystallized in a book called *A Criticism of Japanese Fascism*. This fine work, unparalleled among Japanese writing at the time, was virtually the only work to deplore the course Japan was taking and sound a warning for the future of the world. In Japan at the time, however, freedom of expression was almost non-existent, and distribution and sales of the work were prohibited by the government.

During the decade and a half from the Manchuria Incident, through the China Incident and the Pacific war, and up to Japan's final, abject defeat, the world of writing and ideas in Japan was consistently dominated by a kind of pseudo-nationalism. The prevailing ideas were, in fact, merely a Japanese version of fascism and nazism, masquerading under the guise of love for Japan and the desire to keep its traditions unsullied. It is no wonder that Nyozekan should have found such an intellectual climate intolerable.

The present work, *The Japanese Character,* is a collection of essays which Nyozekan wrote between 1935 and 1938 as a means of correcting such mistakes and misconceptions concerning Japan. "The virtues of the Japanese national character," he said, "are not only mistaken by foreigners, but are frequently misunderstood by the Japanese themselves." To remedy such failings was his chief aim.

Nyozekan sees the natural, guileless society of the time when the *Manyōshū* and *Kojiki* were written as representing all that is most truly "Japanese," and another of his aims was to show that the nationalism and talk of the "Japanese spirit" so widespread in Japan around the time when the book appeared were in fact nothing more than authoritarian ideas imported from the Chinese mainland in ancient times as a means of maintaining political control, or else a kind of absolutist militarism imported from modern Germany and Italy. He wanted to show in a scientific fashion, with concrete illustrations, that the Japanese character is of a broad-minded, natural-

ist, positivist bent, and to bring the fact home to Japanese and foreigners alike.

In order to elucidate the Japanese character it is necessary, of course, not merely to make a broad, general study of history, but to trace the origins, development, and present state of a wide range of particular cultural forms in art, literature, and other fields. This book was put together as a kind of general introduction to the subject, as a first approach to the task of making such a wide, deep study. The author examines the Japanese character, not out of any nationalistic sense of its superiority or exaggerated hankering after the past, but in an exploratory spirit; he seeks to dissect the Japanese outlook, and to lay bare its true nature, from a more international viewpoint than any writers have adopted hitherto.

In 1942, during the hectic days of World War II, the author published a sequel to *The Japanese Character,* then wrote nothing further on the subject until the end of the war. Following Japan's defeat, however, he once more began writing, and produced a succession of new works on Japanese culture and the Japanese character. One of his objects here was to upbraid and hearten the Japanese themselves who, in the humiliation of defeat, had lapsed into nihilism or self-disgust. Another was to throw some light on the subject for the benefit of the more than two million Americans who came to Japan after the war along with visitors from all over Asia and Europe, who were beginning to notice the unique qualities of the Japanese character and culture and to show a desire to study them in more detail.

No one could be better qualified for this task than Hasegawa Nyozekan, and *The Japanese Character,* though one of his earlier works in the field, is undoubtedly one of the best.

LIST OF HISTORICAL PERIODS

Listed below are the names and dates of Japanese historical periods
to which the author makes direct reference in this book.

NARA: 646–794

HEIAN: 794–1185

KAMAKURA: 1185–1333

MUROMACHI (Ashikaga): 1337–1573

SENGOKU: *circa* 1460–1585

MOMOYAMA: 1586–1615

EDO (Tokugawa): 1615–1867

MEIJI: 1868–1912

The
Japanese
Character

I THE JAPANESE CHARACTER

1. The Term "National Character"

The character of a nation, just as that of the individual, determines the general trends of its mental states and actions at a deep-rooted level. However, again like the individual character, it is not something determined before birth as are animal instincts; it is built up over a long period of history, and its formation and growth take place hand in hand with the formation and development of social and cultural forms. Thus it is something which should be constantly cultivated, rather than clung to as an unchanging absolute.

Since different ages demand different traits of both the nation and the individual, this cultivation of character should never be rigid and inflexible. In Japan of the Tokugawa period, for instance, the exclusionist, individualistic traits of the national character were emphasized as a means of maintaining Japan's seclusion, but in the period of the opening of the country which followed the Meiji Restoration the liberal, tolerant traits were in demand to facilitate the introduction of foreign culture, and attempts were made to cultivate the national character to fit in with the new policies.

No generalizations can be made, however, as to the rights and wrongs of these two approaches. Both represented powerful attempts to use the national character for particular purposes, and nothing more. Seclusion was in no sense a product of a racial prejudice of the Japanese—we shall see later just how liberal and tolerant the Japanese have been toward foreigners and foreign culture, par-

3

ticularly foreign religions—but arose solely from a desire to check an actual danger, a danger which made it necessary to carry through exclusion even to the extent of altering the traditional character. The same was true of the demand for the opposite characteristics in the period of modernization from Meiji times on, when the rapid taking-over of foreign culture was a practical necessity and in no sense a departure from a norm.

The cultivation of character requires the imposition of particular thought forms, and the approach to the formulation of those ideas also, as goes without saying, shows variations from age to age. Thus in the mid-Tokugawa period, a movement arose for the revival of the study of the Japanese classics, pushing into the background the Confucianism and Buddhism which had assisted in the cultivation of the Japanese character for so many years. This movement, too, was dictated by fear of pressure from outside forces, which required a remodelling of the feudally divided Japan to form a stronger, more unified nation, which in turn necessitated the resuscitation of a firm national consciousness. The most natural and effective way of achieving this was to have recourse, as a theoretical model, to the type of unified state centering on the national family which had existed in ancient Japan. It was necessary also to keep a check on the power of Confucianism—which had itself contributed to the feudal system—and of the Buddhist temples, which possessed a unifying religious organization closely corresponding to the organization of the feudal state.

Character is usually cultivated by elements of faith and intellect simultaneously, but the emphasis shifts from the one to the other depending on the age, so as to bring into play the particular aspect of character required at the time—which is another reason why it is impossible to pigeonhole national character neatly as one might do with animals. When, in the ancient period of the national religion, a world religion—Buddhism—reached Japan, the Mononobe family, representing the "faith" aspect of the national character, declared

4

that it was blasphemy to bring in a foreign religion where a native belief already existed. The Soga, the "intellectual" side, claimed that there was no reason why Japan should be the only nation to reject a religion deriving from such a civilized country as China. The argument eventually became tied up with the political rivalry between the two factions, but in the end the Japanese, who were then in the process of taking over foreign civilization, accepted the views of the "intellectual" faction. In other words, they cultivated and developed the liberal, tolerant traits in the national character, and they continued to make use of these traits for long afterwards.

A national character is reared by long years of history and complex sets of circumstances; like the individual character, it is brought to its final form gradually, via a succession of errors, failures, and trials, but eventually—again in the same way as the individual character—it comes to show a particular bent in the ways it influences history and deals with its surroundings. This bent, of course, is not, like biological instincts, a set of simple inherited reflexes, being no more than an intellectual and emotional tendency fostered by a particular way of life and nurtured by a particular form of society. Nevertheless, a character that has been fostered by a particular national or social setting over an extremely long period of time does come to form a particular pattern of outlook and behavior, a basic temperament that could almost be called fundamental.

It is in this way that a nation comes to have its own special character by which its ideas and actions are ruled. What is commonly referred to as "national character" is generally conceived of as more specifically ethnological than the type referred to here. However, it would seem doubtful whether, strictly speaking, such a national character can in fact be preserved in the same way as the biological and morphological attributes of the race. Most of the characteristics normally referred to as "national" are in fact no more than intellectual and emotional trends produced by the social forms—national, political, economic, and so forth—amidst which the race has lived

for so long. It would be difficult to deny the existence of such particular trends, amounting almost to a unique temperament, at the basis of every national character, and most historians accept without question that they have a considerable importance in the development of any nation.

This, then, is what is meant by "national character." It is distinguished by the constant and almost inescapable influence it has on the nation's state of mind and actions, irrespective of whether this influence is for good or for bad. In the age before man became conscious of himself, the trend appeared unconsciously and in practical ways, automatically determining the trends of the nation's history, and frequently leading to mistakes both of outlook and action. No character, however admirable it may seem, can be equally adequate to every set of circumstances, and if applied to everything without conscious adaptation is bound to lead to mistakes. Thus awareness of its own national character becomes a practical necessity in a people. Just as the individual needs to reflect on himself, trying to develop his virtues and control his shortcomings, so it is only when a nation awakens to its own character that what it believes to be this character becomes an objective factor in the situation, and the national outlook and behavior can be brought into line with actuality.

To acquire an objective awareness of one's own character is difficult, of course. What makes error particularly easy here is that the difficulty of becoming aware of the processes forming one's own thought often leads to self-deception, making any real reflection on one's own character impossible. This is as true of the nation as of the individual. As a result, most peoples are divided between two completely opposing views of their own character. Thus the English are divided into those who believe themselves to be traditionalist and conservative, and those who believe themselves to be enterprising and progressive. The French, again, include some who think they are radical by nature and others who see themselves as guardians of tradition. In reality, their mental makeup reveals both aspects in

quite pronounced form. In England, it would be hard to say whether liberalism or conservatism was the stronger, and the same is true of radicalism and conservatism in France. The actual national characters of these nations, therefore, is not something determined one way or the other by intellectual outlooks, but should be considered, as a whole, as deriving from a mixture of these characteristics. It can be recognized objectively through examination of their historical trends, attitudes and methods as a race, rather than of any intellectual leanings toward, say, radicalism or conservatism.

In practice, indeed, almost any national character is complex in the extreme, almost self-contradictorily diverse, and races which are like this have a greater potential for evolutionary development than races with undiversified characters closer to the simplicity of animals. In the case of the individual, the man who is "strong against both good and evil" has the most powerful character, and the same is true of national character also. A condition for its development is that all kinds of traits, even diametrically opposed traits, should have developed together, since this means that each trait has a correspondingly complex setting with which it can interact. A character that is set constantly in one direction, as are those of plants and animals, can cope well with one particular set of circumstances, but is powerless with others and is at a very great disadvantage in adapting to the complexities of human history.

The more the character of a nation is capable of development, the more surely it embodies the reverse characteristics as well. One thing, however, should be remembered here. It is that one or the other of these opposing characteristics is always to the fore in the history of the nation, depending on which of them is more necessary in the particular historical setting of the time, and that it exerts a correspondingly powerful effect in giving the national character its particular flavor at that time.

The Japanese of ancient times, for example, showed an extremely internationally-minded, tolerant disposition in their development,

thanks to which they acquired an ancient culture of which they can be proud before the world; yet in the Tokugawa period, as we have already seen, they were given a completely opposite, exclusionist character. In ancient times one aspect of the national character was active, in Tokugawa times another, completely different aspect. This state of affairs does not only apply to widely separated ages, but is quite possible in periods that are close to each other in time. As we have already seen, the national character that appeared in the early Meiji period was completely opposite from that of ten or twenty years previously, nor is it the same as that of today, forty or fifty years later.

The question remains of which was closer to the most permanent aspects of the Japanese character, the aspects preserved throughout these changes. In the period of politically enforced absolute isolation, the absence of the means of development kept the Japanese shut up within their traditional character, but even during this period they worked to effect contact with other cultures by whatever slight means presented themselves, and escaped entirely the exclusionism arising from racial or religious prejudice that affected other countries. The prohibition of Christianity was in no sense a case of national religious exclusionism, but arose purely from the political necessity of countering possible Western colonialism. The methods adopted admittedly showed in some respects a medieval cruelty, but the measures as such were, politically, perhaps unavoidable.

Despite such interruptions, it is safe to say that almost no other people in the world has shown such a readiness to welcome incursions by other peoples and other faiths. This stems from the fact that throughout their long history the Japanese people have made their greatest advances less as a result of their exclusionist, conservative traits than of their conciliatory, progressive traits. So it is the tendency to assimilate, fostered over a long period of history, rather than the tendency to exclude shown in reaction to particular cir-

cumstances, which truly characterizes the national personality. Na-
tionally, racially, and in their religion the Japanese are marked by
tolerance rather than its reverse. This trait, fostered in ancient
times, persisted through the ages until the political requirements of
the Tokugawa period obscured it, and it is for precisely this reason
that the rapid modernization of Japan in post-Meiji times was in no
sense out of the national character.

The Japanese national character, in fact, displays features which
are rather exceptional in an Oriental race. Westerners often speak
of religious intolerance as though it were a characteristic of the
Oriental, deliberately overlooking the cruel religious inquisitions
so common in medieval Europe. Those same Occidentals, when they
first came to Japan, were astonished at the extraordinary tolerance
shown by the Japanese toward other races and religions.

The first European in Japan was Francis Xavier, the missionary
who, at the command of the Pope, came to Japan around the middle
of the sixteenth century. Xavier describes in his writings the religious tolerance of the Japanese. Though in their homes it often happens that disputes arise because of differences of faith between the
generations, the Japanese hold—he explains—that "Men are as
varied as their faces; therefore it is natural that in the service of religion also they should fail to agree in their outlook." He also describes how, during his proselytizing activities in Yamaguchi, he
defeated a Buddhist priest in public debate, to the great delight of
the Japanese audience. Anyone who actually saw what happened, he
says, might have felt as if he were in the universities of Europe; it
was an experience which he constantly recalled with pleasure.

This should be set alongside the welcome accorded by the Japanese to the religions, arts, and sciences of the Asian mainland as
evidence of the nature of the Japanese character—a character which
kept them from falling intellectually and spiritually into the over-
consciousness of racial differences, religious bigotry, and intellec-

9

tual self-satisfaction found in many Oriental races, and which gave their intellectual and spiritual outlook a very naturalistic, realistic, and in this sense modern bent.

2. OBJECTIVE FACTORS AFFECTING THE JAPANESE CHARACTER

As we have just seen, the Japanese are naturalistic and realistic in their intellectual approach. Their emotional outlook also exhibits corresponding features. Thus it is less subjective than objective, less romantic than realistic, less extreme than middle-of-the-way, less grandiloquent than concise, less pretentious than unassuming, less out-of-the-way than commonplace, less heroic than sensible. In short, Japanese emotional attitudes are firmly rooted in everyday life.

In the three sets of factors—natural, economic, and political—which in Japan as in other countries determine the national character, one might well detect elements making these attitudes inevitable. Japan is blessed with the climate, vegetation, etc. typical of the moderate, temperate regions. Her mountains, plains, and rivers similarly exhibit none of the forbidding extremes which one finds on the continent, but tend to the moderate, the delicate, the minute, and the approachable. There are no areas such as are found, for example, in the north of China, nor are there the great conglomerations of mountains and water—as big as two or three Japans put together—which one finds in south China. There are no rivers such as the Yangtsekiang, which would take years to navigate in a raft from source to estuary. A Japanese in China senses in its great plains, where hundreds of miles of land are gathered into one great panorama, and across which winds for hundreds of miles the Great Wall, something he has never experienced in his own country. A people which has been exposed to such things for thousands of years naturally comes to have a special character very different from that

of peoples used to different environments. Economically speaking, too, Japan has a very intensive agriculture unlike the large-scale, rough-and-ready agriculture found elsewhere. There are no places where, as in the U.S.A., one ploughs with tractors great tracts which it would take the best part of a day to go round on foot. It follows that one does not have in Japan the extreme spaciousness of feeling which one finds in these places. Whether this is a good thing or a bad thing, it is true that it is from such things that the national dislike of extremes derives.

Economically, too, the two extremes are avoided: there has been no unequal amassing of wealth through excessive expansion of the economy; there has been neither wealth nor poverty on the grand scale; and the economy has depended—as is illustrated by Japanese agriculture, with its intensive techniques—on quality rather than quantity.

Where political features are concerned, the contrast with the continent is marked in every respect. First, there is the fact that racial differences had already been adjusted in the prehistoric period, so that no large-scale racial disputes have occurred within the historic period. Secondly, there is the fact that the unifying form represented by the clan system took shape in the prehistoric period, and that no internal struggle has occurred to upset that unity. Thirdly, there is the fact that the political unity of the country thereby escaped the trials that beset it in many countries and took the form, from the outset, of a paternalism derived from a view of the nation as one family. Fourthly, since Japan was never subjugated by another nation, political differences were never exacerbated by racial differences. Fifthly, there is the fact that the central authorities never went in for large-scale appropriations of property; on the contrary, the central authorities were concerned, from quite an early date, to control local seizures of land. Sixthly, as a natural outcome of these practical political features, the focus of political unity became at the same time the racial and social focus, which made

impossible any taking-over of the focus of unity by armed might. The successive military governments of Japan were unable to touch the absolute authority of the imperial family as the traditional center; what was more, they found themselves in a dilemma where not to show respect for that tradition would lead to their own ruin, while to show overmuch real respect would similarly endanger their own existence. It was this dilemma that brought about the downfall of the Tokugawa Shogunate, the last of the military governments.

This sixth factor is a natural outcome of the fact that the first political form to come into existence in Japan was a unity based on family ties, a unity which rejected any idea of racial strife. The one thing which most tends to disrupt faith in the national family as the focus, and in the political forms rooted in that faith, is conquest by a foreign nation—which is something that never happened to Japan. Domestic military governments, it goes without saying, never had the power to destroy the focus of the national faith; respect for it was, in fact, a necessary condition for the establishment of their own power.

Without doubt, it was natural, economic, and political factors such as these which gave the Japanese race its moderate nature and its dislike of extremes. Where the pressure of natural forces is too great, man must either submit to them mechanically or seek to overcome them by the force of ideas. In the former case, as in Egypt, man's aim becomes symbolically to imitate nature, and to reproduce its grandeurs; in the latter case, as in China or Russia, man adopts a theoretical approach, transcendental or nihilistic as the case may be, in order to escape from it. In Japan, where such external factors are absent, man accepted nature as it was and developed a disposition that was moderate, averse to extremes and exaggeration, and felt no need for intellectual excitements and evasions. Here lies the basis of the naturalistic and realistic bent of the Japanese character.

Economically as well, Japan was influenced at an early date by exchanges with foreign countries, and its development owed much

to imitation of the more advanced economy and culture of the Chinese mainland. The natural outcome was a tolerant, unassuming attitude to foreigners and their culture; racial prejudices would seem to have been disposed of by the end of the prehistoric period.

Most ancient states would accept foreigners and their methods in the military sphere, but Japan took in large quantities of foreign immigrants in administrative works, as well as in the arts and crafts and the productive industries. In ancient Japan, just as at the time of the Meiji Restoration but for a far longer period—probably from long before the age of the Emperor Sujin, which is recorded as marking the beginning of foreign exchanges, right up to the Nara period —not only administrative affairs but the arts, scholarship and industrial techniques were carried forward under the guidance of naturalized foreigners or their descendants. Accustomed as they were to accepting foreign influence in the form of peaceful cooperation, the Japanese were scarcely likely to be disposed to racial bigotry or prejudice. Nor, as in many ancient empires, were the foreign technicians employed as slaves; on the contrary, they were employed as instructors, and this inevitably encouraged the traditional attitude of reverence for foreigners and foreign cultures already mentioned above. It was for this same reason, probably, that in a later age the first foreign missionaries, "heathen" though they were, were not greeted with contempt and rejection as among other Oriental races. Nor was the reverence servile, but willingly given, so that it did no harm to the national character. Thus even in the age of the Taika Reform—an age of extreme worship of things foreign—Japan demanded to negotiate on equal terms with the great continental Chinese Empire. Phrases such as "From the Emperor of the Land of the Rising Sun to the Emperor of the Land of the Setting Sun," or "The Emperor of the East sends his respects to the Emperor of the West," which occur in diplomatic documents, are well-known examples.

It goes without saying that Japanese political forms contributed

to the formation of such a naturalistic, realistic turn of mind. More-over, one important outcome of the various features of those polit-ical forms already mentioned above was to give the aristocratic class in Japan a peculiar nature of its own. It is common in most countries for the so-called national character to acquire its most strongly char-acteristic flavor in the outlook of the traditional aristocratic class. This is particularly true of the emotional outlook of the race, which the aristocratic class spreads via culture and refines via philosophy, what was originally a purely instinctive psychology being organized into a highly developed political and cultural consciousness and pro-pagated so that the aristocratic psychology eventually colors the whole national character.

The aristocratic class in Japan was, from ancient times, compara-tively unexclusive and progressive. However, this was not, as fre-quently happened in the ancient states of both East and West, because the aristocracy were the descendants of more civilized foreigners, but because, as we have already seen, natural, economic, and polit-ical conditions conspired naturally to make them so. Thus there was no feeling of racial antagonism toward the aristocratic class such as was seen in other countries. There were common features in the psychology of the two sides; the aristocrats, in fact, tended to form an intermediary class of the type seen in the bureaucrats of the Meiji era. From the very outset, the Japanese aristocracy was by way of being, and filling the role of, an intelligentsia.

The political evils and cultural decadence consequent on govern-ment by an aristocracy were as inevitable in Japan as elsewhere. They were particularly marked toward the end of the Heian period, in the period of change-over to government by the military clans, when the special qualities of the preceding period began to disappear, leaving a typical case of relaxed morals and decadent mores. Order and stability disappeared, both in the capital and the provinces, and the aristocratic class became no more than a useless superstructure, a corrupt fog hanging over a chaotic society. Nevertheless, the con-

cept of an aristocracy which they had established in Japan had become so firm a tradition that it was to persist as a name, a way of
thought, and a cultural influence throughout all the succeeding ages
of military rule. The new military "aristocracy" proved ultimately
unable to shake this court aristocracy from its hierarchical and cultural position.

The relationship between the military aristocracy and the courtly
aristocracy was of a kind unknown in other countries. It gave the
Japanese upper classes a peculiar character of their own, in that the
military aristocracy was placed under a social compulsion, as it were,
to imitate the traditional aristocracy. Though one talks of a military
aristocracy, one should remember, of course, that most of its members were originally regional officers of the central aristocracy who
built up their own power in the provinces, became local lords, took
to arms and eventually rose up in opposition to central authority;
they were not foreign warriors of the type, for example, that
brought about the fall of Rome. Thus by the time they came to replace the courtly aristocracy, it could almost be said that the spirit
of their ancestors, lost in the central authority of the time, survived
more strongly, in the form of the "samurai" spirit, among these
powerful families in the provinces. The Minamoto and Taira families, for instance, may remind one of Rome insofar as they were
mercenaries of the central authority who seized power by force of
arms. Yet at the same time they were Japanese; their ancestry lay
in the central aristocracy, and they preserved the spirit of their ancestors in comparatively healthy form. It was this that gave them a
character fundamentally different from that of the aristocracy of
feudal lords in other countries in medieval times.

Because of these special circumstances in the formation of the
military aristocracy, the traditional spirit of the aristocratic class was
carried on even in the age of rule by the provincial aristocracy which
emerged from the purely local powerful families, and gave this
aristocracy in general a respect for the cultural authority of Kyoto.

In China, Confucius had worked to inculcate in the militaristic ruling classes toward the end of the Chou Dynasty a respect for Chou culture, so as to provide an intellectual core for the restoration of order to a chaotic society. In Japan, a more natural process of preservation, in both the political system and the national culture, of the traditions of the Court and the aristocracy meant that the central idea of national order was not lost, however confused the age. And when the collapse of feudal government finally came, this central concept of a traditional order, preserved in both the social system and its culture, became in itself a force working to overthrow the feudal system.

An example demonstrating just how far the traditional aristocratic spirit which developed in Japan was carried on, not only among the military aristocracy, but even among the low-ranking samurai, is found in the story of a robber which is related in the 3 *Okinagusa*. During the Sengoku age, robbers did more or less as they pleased all over the country, but they were particularly rife in the Mino Owari area. One day, a robber arrived at a farmhouse in this area, intent on robbing it. He peered in, and saw a woman boiling some rice gruel. Wanting to see if it was properly cooked, she did not shovel some into her mouth as she might have been expected to do, but took one grain with the tip of a pair of chopsticks, placed it on the lid of the pot, and pressed it with her fingers. Seeing this, the robber was so impressed at the good manners she showed in such a place, with no one to see her, that he went off and left her unharmed. The situation was very different in China, where the concept of *li*, stressed as the formal and spiritual symbol of Chou culture in order to keep order in troubled times, did not, in practice, fulfill its aims. In Japan, examples such as that just given show that its equivalent permeated society down to the humblest peasants—even to robbers in a chaotic age. The same story, one might think, might well occur in any country, but among the many tales told of the provincial samurai in Japan this one is particularly interesting in

that it shows that the same aristocratic sense of propriety extended not merely to the lower-ranking samurai, but down to the very peasants. It is another example showing how the Japanese national character is the property less of a particular class than of the whole nation. Although cultural forms as such may emerge from the upper classes, they permeate right down to the lower classes.

The fact that a political system centering on the emperor should survive as the theoretical source of power, surmounting all domestic upheavals, for more than a thousand years—a system maintained, moreover, without reliance on military force—is a sign of the correspondence between the character of the aristocratic class and that of the nation as a whole.

The special features of a national character are expressed with particular clarity in its literature, and the fact that the aristocratic literature of ancient times can be shown to reveal the same tendencies as have consistently marked the whole literature of the nation affords positive proof of the views just outlined. I shall examine this question briefly in the next section; the point to remember is that, since the peculiar features of the Japanese character were already in evidence in ancient times and would seem to have been retained right up until the present, to understand the typical features of the culture of ancient times is of great help in understanding the basic traits of the national character as a whole which have found such varying modes of outward expression from age to age.

3. Japanese Literature and the Japanese Character

If we have so far treated the naturalistic and realistic bent of the Japanese people as a characteristic of the aristocratic class, it is because of the almost total preoccupation of ancient history and literature with the life of that class. In practice, however, the same character should be considered as having belonged to society as a whole.

Admittedly, our only source of knowledge of the most primitive national outlook is through history recorded after the establishment of the outlook of the aristocratic class, but since, as we have seen, the Japanese aristocracy, unlike its Western counterparts, was not a foreign entity alien to the people as a whole, it is only natural that it should have shared its basic features with the rest of the nation.

The scarcity of heroic myths in Japan stems from the same reason. The gods of the Japanese mythical age all possessed human emotions; the loftier the god, the more this was apparent. The heroic gods tended to be relegated to second place, and were frequently criticized from a purely human standpoint.

This may well represent a conscious outlook expressed in histories compiled, after the establishment of a national state, in order to express the official outlook of that state. Although they were records of popular tradition, it seems that these traditions were handed down chiefly by the organization of *kataribe*, and it is obvious that they had a didactic significance. Yet the fact that the gods were human in nature shows that no need was felt to make the outlook of the upper classes any different from that of the common people. It is true, of course, that following the introduction of Chinese learning its influence created a tendency in making histories to adopt a ruling-class attitude more typical of the continent. The *Nihon Shoki* is the first of these, but it is significant that this Chinese-style history was preceded by the *Kojiki*, in which the old traditions were duly set down. The *Nihon Shoki* is, as it were, a history "for show." Motoori Norinaga pointed out this fact, calling the *Kojiki* a history "in the Japanese spirit" *(Yamato-gokoro)* and the *Nihon Shoki* a history "in the Chinese spirit" *(Kara-gokoro)*. Motoori's exclusive championship of the *Kojiki* is, of course, rather exaggerated, but his view must be considered correct in so far as it saw the *Kojiki* as an expression of the Japanese character. And that character, as Motoori himself pointed out, was naturalistic and realistic.

The absence of racial prejudice among the Japanese is similarly

18

borne out by the *Kojiki* myths. In a history which lays specific emphasis on the unity of the Yamato race, the myths of the Izumo race are set down in all fairness, and the power of the Izumo race clearly described. What is more unusual for a myth is the fact that its amalgamation with the Yamato tribe takes place through diplomatic negotiations. According to modern historians, of course, both the Yamato people and the Izumo people belonged to the same race, the distinction between them being purely political, but even if one accepts this, the fact that such an opposition should have been resolved by peaceful means undoubtedly played its part in determining the national character.

The later negotiations with the three Korean kingdoms were undoubtedly intended to lead to peaceful exchanges between Japan and the peninsula. The Japanese forces were, in fact, driven out by those of T'ang China, and in the reign of the Emperor Tenji, battle was actually joined with the T'ang forces on the Korean coast, but once Japan had withdrawn from Korea she promptly began diplomatic exchanges with T'ang China and sent frequent envoys. In this way, she managed not merely to save the national face but actually to gain prestige.

It is quite typical of the Japanese character that the same, eminently realistic approach should have been fostered throughout all the long history of national development from the prehistoric age on into the Nara and Heian periods. One can detect this national character at work in the *Kojiki*, which clothes the ancient traditions in the garb of history, and in poems in the *Kojiki*, the *Nihon Shoki*, and the *Manyōshū*, where they appear in verse form. Although the *Nihon Shoki* is the product of an age already considerably under the influence of Chinese ideas, it still reveals distinctive features of the national character, while the *kana* literature of the Heian period, when a distinctive Japanese culture emancipated from the influences of the Continent at last emerged, shows these Japanese features still more clearly.

Aristocratic society in the period before the development of a Japanese script was restricted to a literature expressed entirely in foreign modes brought in via the Chinese script and Chinese learning. In this, they were still more handicapped than the aristocracy and scholars of medieval Europe who had to rely for literary and philosophical expression on Latin and French. True, there were some aristocrats of the day who could write Chinese almost better than the Chinese themselves. Nevertheless, it remains impossible to create one's own literature in another language. They tried, accordingly, giving the Chinese characters Japanese readings, and later also tried using the characters purely as phonetic symbols (this was probably an achievement of the *fumibe*, naturalized foreigners who were responsible for keeping records for the Court). The eventual result was the creation of the *kana* syllabary. Thus the Japanese began to write Japanese with *kana*, and for the first time Japan acquired a written literature of its own (the *Kojiki*, which might seem to be an example of this, should really be classified as oral literature).

An interesting phenomena here is that when *kana* literature appeared it inherited the general tendencies of the ancient oral literature. The *Kojiki* was not compiled until after the development of Chinese studies in Japan, but the work belongs essentially to the age of oral literature, since it came into being when the Emperor Temmu —in order to set to rights the ancient oral traditions, which had fallen into confusion during the reign of the Emperor Gemmei— issued an edict under which Hida no Are recited ancient records in the ancient language and a Chinese scholar set them down in Chinese characters. It includes a large number of poems, and was almost certainly recited with a kind of rhythmic syllabification like the later *katarimono* (ballads). Nowadays, the same kind of material would probably be recorded.

Thus the age in which the oral traditions in the *Kojiki* were set down in Chinese characters represents a transitional period in which Japanese literature had lost its verbal tradition, yet had not succeeded

in emerging in new form, written in a native script. Literature in Japan at that time consisted of Chinese poems and fragments of Chinese prose only. Moreover, it was written in a foreign script in a foreign mode of expression, the only traces of anything really Japanese being found in practical documents such as letters, diaries and political papers. The *Kaifuso* and *Honcho Monzui* are imitations of the Chinese anthologies pure and simple, their only value lying in the extreme skill with which the imitation is done. To look to them for any expression of the Japanese character is, as the Japanese say, like climbing a tree to catch a fish. The one work, even of this age, in which the Japanese character finds expression is the *Manyōshū*, which uses Chinese ideographs simply as phonetic symbols; the poems in it which are expressions of a national awareness are rich in typically Japanese traits.

However, with the Heian period the emergence of a Japanese literature written in *kana* script saw a sudden, clearly-defined return to the oral tradition in the ancient language, which it resembled in its whole literary approach. The intermediary age of foreign literature might have been completely forgotten, so little influence from it is apparent. In this, the new literature is perhaps reminiscent of the literature of the Renaissance in Europe.

This new literary trend, unlike the prose and poetry in Chinese, which had depended chiefly on the subjective or purely imaginative, sought after direct objectivity. The term "Japanese character" used in reference to Heian literature should apply, not to the decadent life which is its subject, but to the character discernible in the human emotions present beneath the surface of that life, and to the literary determination to see that life whole. As I have said above, purely intellectual works can be produced by the imitation of foreign characteristics or by the pursuit of logic, but works of art are also the unconscious products of self-revelation. Thanks to the appearance of the *kana* phonetic syllabary, the Japanese at last acquired a means of expressing their own feelings and emotions almost as

freely as in speech, so that their character now received direct expression through literature. This is particularly so with the works in diary form, which were, one supposes, not intended for public inspection; they accordingly occupy a very important position in literature, and afford extremely valuable material for the historian.

This literature is, of course, aristocratic, yet it shows a similarity to modern European literature in constituting a direct reflection of the life of the age, and in displaying a similarly modern self-awareness. Such a self-awareness invariably crops up at turning-points in history, and this ancient literature was itself a herald of the transition from aristocratic government to government by the warrior clans. The fact that such self-awareness finds expression in literature means that the time has come for using self-awareness as a means to self-renovation; indeed, government by the warrior clans—as even the pro-imperial Kitabatake Chikafusa pointed out—was an inevitable development which had been prepared for by the aristocratic government itself and which signified an escape from national decadence.

The ancient literature which gave artistic voice to these symptoms of self-awareness was written almost entirely by women, and even such a massive work as the *Eiga Monogatari*, believed to be the first history written in Japanese, is said to have been penned by a feminine hand. In this extraordinary phenomenon, probably unparalleled anywhere else in the world, lies another clue to the Japanese character. Its causes were, no doubt, complex, but the chief of them would seem to have been that the aristocracy had lost its role as an intelligentsia, and that the role passed into the hands of its womenfolk. Since the collapse of the Mononobe, the aristocracy of ancient Japan had been dominated chiefly by government officials occupying a position similar to that of the bureaucracy of Meiji times, with naturalized foreigners in charge of the technical aspects of administration. In time, imitation of the continental system had led to the selection of government officials by written examination,

22

and official and private schools developed in order to prepare for these examinations. The practical offices of state were left to these administrative officials, and the higher-ranking aristocracy had nothing to do but indulge in struggles for positions at the Court. The high-ranking male aristocracy became a leisured class with nothing but its aristocratic culture, while those of lower rank became glorified clerks; neither of them were fitted for the role of intellectuals. Those who happened to have neither wealth nor position were perhaps in a position to become the intellectual class and to be active in the literary field, but the continuing imitation of continental models even after the development of *kana* made them feel it below their dignity to write in it, and they persisted in penning a foreign tongue; the result was that they still had no means of expressing their real feelings in their own language.

With their womenfolk it was different. Despite the fact that Chinese learning was considered a masculine province taboo to women, the social position of women in the aristocracy of ancient times was such that they acquired, in practice, a good grounding not only in the Japanese classics but in the Chinese classics also. Traditionally, too, the position of women was quite strong, as is apparent from the number of powerful women which Japanese society had been producing ever since the most ancient times. Though it seems unlikely that they were educated for particular positions as were the men of the aristocracy who were destined to become public officials, they received a very liberal and very high-quality education. It even seems to have included instruction in Chinese characters and Buddhist learning, which in theory were supposed to be subjects too stern for the weaker sex. The *Bunka Shūrei Shū*, a contemporary collection of Chinese prose and verse, includes work by a woman of the Ōtomo family, while the *Keikokushū* contains a poem by the Princess Uchiko, daughter of the Emperor Saga. The latter includes phrases such as: "How can I bear to sleep alone? Nothing can distract my mind from thoughts of love."—which suggests that liberality in the

upbringing of women was not confined to the ladies-in-waiting only.

The women of the aristocracy who found themselves in this type of position must have been something like the intelligentsia of today —free, that is, to criticize, but without practical responsibility—and were thus in a position to develop the intellectual and amatory pursuits to their highest perfection. Moreover, where the expression of feeling was concerned, they were accustomed to using the *kana* syllabary in which it was possible to write freely in Japanese. It was no wonder, therefore, that the women of the age should outstrip the men, who were restrained by their Chinese learning from more naturally Japanese ways of thinking and expression, and reap to themselves the glory of founding the first true Japanese literature.

The "modern" approach which this women's literature of ancient times shows in its approach to description, though admittedly made possible by this peculiar position of women, was undoubtedly a continuation of the Japanese character which had existed since prehistoric times. The same approach to description is apparent, though in a very primitive, simple form, in the *Kojiki*, which was originally verbal literature, and in the *Tale of Genji*—though a tendency to literary over-refinement makes the latter somewhat obscure in places—but with the *Eiga Monogatari* the style is plainer, and the descriptions in the well-chosen historical anecdotes with which the text is interspersed are, allowing for differences in the language, completely modern.

It is not certain how far this type of literature was known to the ordinary people at the time. However, it is clear that it spread with great rapidity among aristocratic society, and it is possible, thus, that its principal contents reached the lower classes in the form of verbally-transmitted tales. It was in this way that the name of Hikaru Genji ("Shining Genji") became a byword among the common people throughout the middle ages and on into modern times.

One thing worthy of special note is that the author of *Tale of Genji*, which is reputed to be very decadent in its content, was in

fact an extremely strict-minded woman. One is reminded of certain phenomena in modern European literature: of Dickens, that exaggerated exponent of the bourgeois English mentality who was at the same time its sternest critic; of Zola, a portrayer of the most decadent aspects of French life who was himself an ardent believer in the spirit; of Chekhov, the supreme exponent of a thoroughgoing Russian pessimism who in actual life was a thoroughgoing optimist, strictly upright in his morals and in his actual behavior, devoted to his specialist profession and his literature throughout his life, the man who married his beloved when death was already in sight. As such examples clearly show, modern literature is a literature of self-awareness. Not only did Murasaki Shikibu come close to such modern literature in her *Tale of Genji*, but in her own attitude to life as well she was close to the healthy modern man.

She was not, however, a mere freak, impossibly ahead of her times, but represented a development of the same Japanese character that had been in process of cultivation since prehistoric times. The Japanese have always managed to take over foreign culture in an imitative fashion yet at the same time, sometimes even discarding the borrowings, to think and act according to their own unique character and eventually to create their own unique culture. The Nō drama is another example of this; although it incorporates forms copied from continental culture, it has much that is quite unique in its literary content, while the still more Japanese *kyōgen* farces, which the Nō originated in order to give unmistakable expression to unequivocally Japanese sentiments, are similar in their literary approach to the humorous literature of modern Europe.

In the Tokugawa period, the literature at first assumed pseudo-classical forms, but around the Genroku era, when the dissemination of reading matter was still inadequate, a kind of visual literature emerged in the form of the Kabuki, in the same way as the Nō and *kyōgen* but on a larger scale and in a much more typically Japanese form. The Kabuki, again, was not content until it had developed

25

away from the "continentally" grotesque approach of the historical plays toward the modern, purely Japanese approach of the domestic dramas. In the same way, with the development of printed literature in the form of the popular novel, there was a shift from romantic translations or adaptations in a kind of degraded "Chinese" style toward a more Japanese, naturalistic and realistic type of literature which was written, moreover, in a style closer to the spoken language.

The Japanese character, basically consistent from ancient up to modern times, gave a similar consistency to Japanese literature. Just as in Heian times the *Kojiki* and other similar literature represented a kind of renaissance—a return to the oral literature of earlier times —so Tokugawa literature from the Genroku era onward was a renaissance harking back to Heian times and its earlier antecedents. In turning back to Heian and earlier literature, the studies of the *12,13* Japanese classics *(kogaku)* made by Keichū, Mabuchi, Norinaga, and their followers parted company with Buddhism and Confucianism, attempting a reappraisal of the Japanese character in their search for a spiritual basis for the new, unified state required by the age. By reference to the myths, *kogaku* set out to show that the basic features of the Japanese character had been laid down along certain lines in the prehistoric period, and to prove academically that the national character since the formation of the state had been a consistent development of those features. The academic approach adopted by *kogaku* is still relevant today in so far as it attempts to define the Japanese character, not in terms of intellectual concepts brought in from abroad, but via the medium of Japan's own history and literature.

II THE TRADITIONAL CHARACTERISTICS
OF JAPANESE CIVILIZATION

I

Japanese civilization, as I see it, can be described as a "civilization of everyday life." The expression of civilization in terms of human feeling is art, and just as this form of expression tells the truth about individual nature with a minimum of falsification, so the truth about a national character can best be found in the art which is the expression of its sensibility.

Japanese art is remote from the kind of esthetics popular in modern Germany which considers art to be the expression of an independent life of its own, a life which transcends ordinary human existence. All the fine arts of Japan are intended for use in everyday life, and in that sense partake of the nature of both fine art and decorative art. Although some Japanese painting and sculpture may seem to deal in transcendental terms with purely intellectual forms such as are represented by the terms idea, consciousness, thought, faith and so on, these were all taken over from Chinese art, and there was no original creation in this sphere. Any attempt to Japanicize them at once had recourse to an artistic sensibility based on the values of actual, everyday life. In this way, for example, the painting originally brought from China developed into the Japanese-style *Yamato-e*. In contrast to the usual idea of a "pure" art which develops in contradistinction to the ideas and emotions of daily life itself, Japanese art tended to be a development of the feeling for ordinary life. In Japanese art there is none of the "pure art" of the West. A Japanese picture does not create, within a frame, an independent

27

esthetic realm of its own, but is an instrument for the beautification of the whole surroundings in which it is placed. Thus even in the largest and wealthiest residence in Japan one would never find a hall with large numbers of pictures hung on the walls. Not only is a picture considered as one element in a setting which includes the whole room and the garden, but it may also be treated as one element contributing to a particular frame of mind for a particular occasion. For a happy occasion, a cheerful scroll is hung in the alcove, for a sad occasion a melancholy scroll. Pictures are seen, in short, only in relation to life itself.

The same is true to a certain extent, of course, of the painting and sculpture of every country. It is a Western idea, however, that the true development of art takes place when it is freed from such considerations and passes on to the expression of the "artistic consciousness" as such. Japanese art makes no attempt whatsoever to reach this point. It is the same with music: purely Japanese music is not an art of sound for its own sake, but is always associated with some literary content expressive of the realities and emotions of ordinary life. There is no Japanese music other than what would be called, in the West, "program music." In the dance, too, the Japanese dance is not a rhythm of dynamic lines pure and simple, but a rhythm of dynamic lines expressing the facts and emotions of life—or rather, a refinement of the lines of life itself.

This term "life" used in reference to Japanese art means, literally, the ordinary, everyday life of the Japanese people, and not an abstract "life" with some extra, theoretical significance. In the West also, modern times brought a new emphasis on "life" in art and ethics, an attempt to restore the human being to his rightful place from which he had been displaced as a result of medieval criteria which had restricted human life. Nietzsche's Superman was one example of the intellectual exaltation of life in this sense. The exaltation of the instinctive life, known by some at the time as "instinctivism," depended, in the long run, on an intellectual concept of

"life as such" created by a vision of an age in which life, hitherto repressed by medievalism, would make a spontaneous leap forward. "Life" in Japanese art is quite different; it is a result of the controlling of the instinctive impulses of life, a rephrasing of everyday, human life so as to achieve a new refinement of its spiritual and material forms. Toward the end of the Meiji era, there was a group of intellectuals in Japan who imported a German-style "intellectual" view of life under the slogan of "the esthetic life," but this had no overall influence even on literature, much less on art as a whole.

At the same time, however, Japanese art displayed none of the ideas typified by the moral view of art which arose as a reaction to this modern trend. Admittedly, the taking over of the ideas of Confucianism and Buddhism was a feature of Japanese literature from the earliest times, and in the middle ages in particular not only literature and history but the whole of art was colored by it—Nō drama, for instance, was a fairly extreme case of the tendency—but this was only inevitable when one considers that the priesthood had a monopoly of literature at this period. And even here the *kyōgen*, which sprang from the same stock as Nō, displayed a different nature.

2

That Japanese civilization is a civilization of daily life can be deduced from the particular type of sensibility which is manifest in Japanese cultural forms in all their aspects. To put conclusions first, I believe that the principle underlying these cultural forms is the control of feeling.

What is meant here by the control of feeling is the "civilized" control, via organic human and social forms of life, of all the instinctive, impulsive life requirements such as are sometimes referred to as the "desire for survival," the "desire for power," and so on. This does

. not imply biological regression or atrophy, but a refinement of the sensibility so as to give a higher intensity of emotion to all cultural phenomena, whether spiritual or physical.

There may be objections to this argument if it is considered only in the abstract, but in reference to the actual manifestations of Japanese culture, this process of "control" is apparent wherever one looks. A particularly marked instance of it is the simplicity of line and sparing use of color in purely Japanese painting. It has been argued that this type of sensibility derives from the absence of any excessively stimulating or overbearing elements in nature as it is known in Japan. It seems likely, however, that it also derives to a great extent from the social and political forms evolved by the Japanese people. Not only the difference of nature in Japan from nature on the continent, but differences from the continent in political and social forms also have had an undoubted influence on the Japanese sensibility. Whatever the reasons for it, however, the difference as such is indisputable.

The "feeling" which I have spoken of as controlled refers comprehensively to the senses, emotions, sentiments, and so on—all of which, of course, act in interrelation to produce what I have referred to as "sensibility." Dance in the West leaps from point to point, and in joining these points together produces a form which is controlled by a type of esthetic law; however, the movement from point to point is *in itself* the expression of no sensibility—or rather, there are no sensuous restrictions on the line of the movement. To put it in other words, there is a "Gestalt" beauty, but no beauty in the linear movements which make up the form itself. The lines appear as lines of movement and not as lines of emotion.

Japanese gardens, unlike the flat, geometrical, Italianate gardens of the West, are "natural" and three-dimensional, but they do not, in the manner of Western landscape gardening, set out to imitate nature life-size, but to reproduce it in miniature. The "tray garden" *(bonkei)* is, of course, the extreme example of this approach, but

the ordinary Japanese garden is essentially the same. Where the Western garden may try to reproduce hills and valleys life-size, its Japanese counterpart sets out to reproduce the feeling of nature in a small-scale form. This too can lead to a kind of formalism, with conventions governing the way natural scenery is scaled down and specifications for various miniature "natural features," each with its own name (see, for instance, the *Sakuteiki*, an early manual on gardening by Kujō Yoshitsune). This constant control naturally has the effect of keeping Japanese cultural forms small. Japanese culture, accordingly, is sometimes thought of as showing the properties typical of an "island" or "pigmy" culture. Either way, it has undoubtedly undergone not an expanding growth but an inner evolution.

Here is another reason for calling Japanese civilization a civilization of actual life, since life itself similarly encounters limitations in every direction. To break down these limitations by force of instinct or impulse is not merely the destruction of an irrelevant morality: it is the destruction of life itself. The Japanese artistic sensibility is based on the principle of control of the senses in accordance with these limitations on life. Japanese civilization is a great compendium of cultural phenomena created on this principle. Just as Japanese vocal music has neither bass nor soprano—both extremes are restricted, and everything depends instead on the "suppression," as it were, of the voice—so Japanese civilization, in the same sense, "suppresses" the senses.

It may be noted here, too, that just as Japanese civilization tailors art, as it were, to everyday life, so many aspects of everyday life are raised to the level of art. A case in point is the so-called "martial arts." Every "martial art" of course implies military force, but the Japanese have raised them to an artistic level unknown in any other country. Whether in fencing, or archery, or *kemari*, the forms remind one in almost every case of the dance. In *kemari*, for instance, artistic "props" are specified, the ball is kicked to the

reciting of poems, and even the cries emitted by the players are laid down. This kind of thing probably came to Japan from India or China, but one doubts whether it was done so artistically there; either way, it has died out there, whereas in Japan it has been developed artistically and still survives to this day.

There can be no other country, again, which has raised military weapons such as the sword to such a high artistic level. In other countries, considerable artistry is lavished on the trappings of swords, but in Japan the blade itself is regarded as a work of art. This requires a completely Japanese type of sensibility, and is an indication of the extreme delicacy of that sensibility. It is not enough that the sword should be sharp. This is not forgotten, of course, but artistic interest also is found in all kinds of features such as the curve of the blade and the texture. A foreigner sees in a sword only something for use against an enemy, and the most artistic sword only inspires him with unpleasant associations. However, even a Japanese with no special interest in swords will forget a sword's lethal aspect and appreciate it for its artistry, just as he would a piece of fine art. This, I believe, is a characteristic manifestation of Japanese culture.

It is the same with archery. Archery in the sense of firing an arrow at a target exists in the West too, but the feeling is completely different. In Japan, the movements of firing the arrow are treated throughout almost as though they were a dance. Unless one goes through the right artistic motions, even a hit is not a "real" hit. It is said, too, that if the artistic motions are perfect, one will hit the target—a claim which is borne out in practice.

The Japanese sensibility, thus, is delicate to the point of regarding even military techniques as art. The same sensibility is applied to everyday life as to art, so that even ceremonies directly bound up with everyday living are extremely highly developed. A good example is the tea ceremony, which is a transformation into art of the ordinary everyday business of making and drinking tea. That the Japanese should have made an art with such a close bearing on their

everyday lives is a proof of how practical is their approach to culture, and of how it avoids the excessively grotesque and stimulating. It is for the same reason that Japanese architecture exhibits the three characteristics which I have already mentioned—moderation, plainness, and restraint.

As an intellectual theory, the same ideas existed in China, which produced various writings on the subject that were of course passed on to Japan. In China, however, they did not take root in the daily lives of the people in the same way as in Japan. The works of Confucius make a great deal of the idea of *li*. The *li* of the *Analects* is, indeed, a fine concept, quite unlike the formalistic ideas of later days, but before long, the spirit of Confucius was lost, and all that was left was an empty idea, the appearance without the substance. The spirit of the tea ceremony, it is said, lies in the way it displays a delicate sensibility without giving way to mere form. In archery and in fencing likewise, the refining of them into a form, rather than merely empty formalism, meant perfecting in the highest degree the art of using the bow and arrow and the sword. So with the tea ceremony: its appeal lies in the fact that it has the very practical aim of developing to perfection the appreciation of tea-drinking. Things are developed, in other words, not as something out-of-the-way, but as a discipline for practical behavior. This is yet another result of the dislike of the Japanese character for extremes.

This also means, of course, that things Japanese seem small-scale, lacking the majesty of things continental. They lack the broad sweep. The Japanese sensibility, like Japanese agriculture, is cultivated with terrific intensity. There is nothing to overwhelm the viewer—all kinds of similar failings could be listed if one cared to do so, since virtues are inevitably accompanied by corresponding vices.

One danger, of course, is the tendency to formalization and adherence to prescribed patterns, and in practice every aspect of Japanese culture displays, as a means of avoiding this pitfall, a tendency to deny formalism and an insistence that mere forms should be

33

transcended. This is found, for example, in the philosophy of the
tea ceremony, which is in one sense the supreme example of the
lapse into formalism. Thus Japanese civilization is not, as it might
at first seem, a civilization of unconscious repression. Either way,
given the choice, the Japanese still prefer the expression of the
Japanese temperament—the moderate, impartial, and sensitive
approach which does not merely touch the surface of things but
delves into every last hidden corner—to the unnecessarily grandiose
or to unnecessarily overbearing displays of power. Japan could never
produce anything so wildly romantic as other countries, or so big for
the sake of bigness as, say, ancient Egypt and modern America, and
it is better that it should not. From a practical point of view it is
correct, I believe, to see as most truly Japanese those things in Japanese culture—whether intellectual, moral, or formal—which display the characteristics of moderation, simplicity, and restraint
apparent since ancient times. The "failings"—the smallness, the
lack of power, the "obviousness"—are really not failings but inevitable results of the essential compactness of Japanese life itself, of
the temperateness of the climate, and of the absence in Japanese
society of violent clashes such as marked the history of other nations.
There has been no need to terrify or overwhelm, no need to dazzle.

3

Another characteristic of Japanese civilization with a bearing on the
traits we have just been discussing is the fact that it is truly "national," in the sense that it is of the whole people. Since, moreover,
this has been true of Japanese civilization from antiquity right up to
modern times, this characteristic can justifiably be referred to as
"traditional."

Japanese art, to take only one example, has revealed a consistent
national sensibility from ancient times up to the present. In Japanese

art history, therefore, there is nothing that corresponds precisely to the Renaissance of the West. Japanese literature of the Genroku era is sometimes linked with the post-Renaissance humanism and naturalism of the West, but, as we shall see later, modern literature in Japan as typified by that of the Genroku era—though similar in that it marked a return to the classics—was a return to the native classics and not those of another nation, a return not to Greece but to the self. Moreover, medieval Japan possessed in every sphere cultural forms which were "modern" in nature precisely because they carried on the traditions of the ancient culture. The "samurai culture" of the middle ages did not represent, as did the medieval culture of Europe, the inheriting of a universal cultural tradition derived from Rome, with a corresponding disappearance of native cultures; it was not a complete departure from the line of ancient Japanese civilization, but merely a new set of cultural forms reflecting changes in the political and cultural forms of Japan as a whole.

Admittedly, specialist studies of specific aspects of its culture will reveal in medieval Japanese civilization details which distinguish it from both ancient and modern times. Nevertheless, there is a consistent thread running through it; it did not mean a process of shifting first from an international civilization to a national one and then back again. Although Japan's acquisition of a high level of culture in ancient times naturally involved all the changes in cultural forms consequent on the incursion of a continental civilization, yet even in the age of worship of things continental the nature of the indigenous culture enabled it, by the Heian period, to emerge from the realm of imitation and create purely Japanese cultural forms, giving birth to a truly Japanese literature, art, and architecture. Japan since the Meiji Restoration has posed a new problem here, yet once again the real question is that of how Western civilization will be Nipponicized; one thing that seems certain is that Japan will not stop at out-and-out imitation of the West.

Whatever may happen in the future, it is true that in the past

35

Japan maintained a consistent general trend throughout its civilization, retaining always the love of restraint which we have already seen as characteristic. The reason for this consistency, as should be obvious, is that there was no change in the central core around which culture developed. A civilization, basically speaking, takes shape at the center of the national organization, and its various cultural forms are fashioned according to the sensibilities of those who stand at the center. In the other countries of East and West, the heart of civilization in this sense—both the race and the class which constituted it—changed frequently. The change from one dynasty to another in the history of those countries oftener than not represented a shift in the center of civilization as well; it not infrequently happened, in extreme cases, that the cultures before and after the shift represented entirely different traditions, both racially and in their content. Japan, however, has had a single, constant focus throughout historical times. In the warrior age, the nation's center shifted from one district to another, and evolved modes of expression based on a new spirit, yet as we shall see later the essence of Japanese civilization preserved the same basic line. As a result, whatever elements were introduced from foreign cultures, the cultural attitude which took them over remained consistent in itself, and Japanese culture as a whole retained its original characteristics. At no time was it possible that in Japan, as in China, the ancient civilization could have come to a dead halt.

It is dangerous to try to understand the special quality of Japanese civilization according to a logic deduced from the growth of Western civilization. For example, the kind of process whereby Greek civilization was inherited by Rome, and Roman civilization in turn spread to other countries, is unknown in Japan. Similarly, the way in which European civilization in the Middle Ages declined in the sectionalized feudal states and developed in the cities which had developed along more international lines finds only a few parallels in the development of Japanese civilization, and even these must

be drawn with great reservations. Japan had nothing to correspond to the international guild towns which were the centers and moulds of medieval civilization in Europe.

Even earlier, the ancient state in Japan was vastly different from the state in other parts of the world. The very soil in which civilization grew was different. It is true that the ancient Japanese state had a colony in Korea, and that the southwestern and northeastern parts of the country were in a sense even remoter than colonies, yet the state of Yamato as such had eliminated racial dissension as early as the prehistoric period and was bound by its religion into a harmonious family relationship; nor did subsequent history produce any conquest or revolution to shatter that first faith. Accordingly there were no racial struggles or switches in political or other forms of rule such as occurred in continental countries, and the conditions did not exist whereby Japanese civilization might have acquired the characteristics which inevitably appear in such nations—the love of the grandiloquent, the domineering, the over-detailed—which are the mark of the conqueror. In Japan there grew up, instead, a civilization of social and individual restraints which was the very antithesis of these continental traits. The very fact that the other ancient civilizations of both East and West derived from towns surrounded by military ramparts, whereas ancient Japanese civilization grew up in towns open to the outside world, is in itself suggestive of the essential difference between the two types of civilization.

Many different reasons can doubtless be found for the fact that the capital city in the central state of ancient Japan did not, as in the other countries, take the form of a walled city. Important among them, however, is the fact that in ancient Japan the forms of the state were already in nationwide existence—as is shown by the fact that already a clan system apportioned the central power throughout the various parts of the nation, local tributes to the state being collected into official storehouses located within the various provinces. Thus the ancient Japanese state, unlike that of China, did

not consist solely of a central, fortified town but was a national entity embracing both town and country. For the same reason, transplanted foreign culture was not concentrated in one central city but was spread widely throughout the provinces. The Chinese and Korean immigrants who were brought into the country in large numbers by the state—principally as a means of introducing learning, techniques, and industry—were distributed all over the country, in order to encourage the development of the provinces. In the same way, the temples which played such an important part in the spreading of civilization from ancient times on were in ancient times built at the state's rather than their own expense. This project was designed not merely to strengthen the power of the state but also, as with the regional distribution of foreign immigrants, to spread civilization throughout the whole nation.

4

The fact that ancient Japanese civilization, unlike that of the Oriental mainland, was not a civilization of the walled city is important in any attempt to ascertain the characteristics, and thus the original nature, of Japanese civilization. It is also relevant to the question of how far ancient Japanese civilization evolved on a class basis and how far on a broader national basis.

It goes almost without saying, of course, that in ancient, medieval, and modern times alike culture developed around the large cities; the level of a country's civilization depends, in the long run, on the level of civilization reached in its towns. Throughout all ages, it is the towns that have provided the headquarters of the ruling class, and insofar as a country's culture arises and develops in its towns it is, obviously, the culture of that class. A vital question here, however, is the nature of the ruling class, since on this depends the nature of the culture itself.

The ancient civilizations of both East and West grew up, as it

were, within the superstructure of the nation, separated by a large gap from the lower strata of society; indeed, the difference between the world within the walled city and the world without was a difference between civilization and barbarism.

In modern civilization too, a gap between the civilizations of town and country is of course unavoidable, and the level of a country's civilization must be determined by a summing-up of the whole. However, the discrepancy that existed between town and country in ancient times was so great that such a summing-up was impossible. The fact that modern Western civilization is by its very nature a civilization of the whole people stems from the fact that the "ruling class" which built up the civilization of the towns was the bourgeoisie. It was this class which broke down the old forms—the systems of rank and class, characteristic of feudal government, which rendered the people as a whole impotent politically and consequently culturally—and brought political, and hence cultural, power within the reach of the masses; even when it, in its turn, came to enjoy the privileges of a ruling class, the culture of the bourgeoisie remained a culture that was truly national.

Any inquiry into the character of ancient Japanese civilization requires, thus, a knowledge of the nature of the ruling class that built it up. It is impossible to apply historical principles deduced from the processes whereby civilizations of kings, emperors and aristocracies came into being within the framework of the ancient civilizations of the West. They cannot, at least, be applied without major reservations.

In almost all civilizations of the world, cultural forms were first created exclusively by statesmen—i.e., the ruling class—within the castle towns. For example, the cultural forms of ancient Egypt, typified by its vast, grotesque buildings, were not expressions of the cultural sensibility of the tens of millions of inhabitants of the Nile valley, but of the civilization of their rulers, which came into existence above their heads.

The civilization of ancient Japan also centered on the towns, and was also a civilization of the ruling class. However, just as there were no walls about the towns, so there were no obstacles to the spread of city civilization. There was provincial distribution of civilization, and there were provincial elements, on the other hand, in the central civilization (perhaps one should say that these were less "provincial" elements than the expression of a more general, national consciousness). The presence of such features in the central civilization is apparent in every sphere—history, literature, and art alike—but they are particularly evident in the approach to history, which will serve well to illustrate the point in question.

The need to make a national history of Japan was undoubtedly first felt under the stimulus of ideas transmitted from China, and the way in which historical awareness is supported by moral ends in particular is characteristically of Chinese origin. However, the first history made in practice was a record of oral traditions, set down for the most part in the original language. Though the idea of compiling histories was taken over from China, there was a world of difference between the Japanese approach to history and the Chinese —or at least that of Confucianism. The history compiled by the imperial household was aimed to "remove what was false and establish what was true" in the "lives of the emperors and ancient traditions handed down in various families," and to "study the old oral traditions." These popular oral traditions embodied all kinds of varying opinions, though records of them were probably handed down in the families of the aristocracy.

This is just the reverse of the method adopted by Chinese historians of the Chou Dynasty, who rejected popular traditions and based history on a completely new, ethical approach. In Japan, the national history compiled in practice was based on traditions orally transmitted by the people themselves. Undoubtedly, of course, all kinds of legends unconnected with the imperial family were weeded out in the process of drawing up the history, but the result was not

an account of the ethics and ethical legislation of an imperial state
such as is found in the *Shu-ching*, but a history of national traditions *14*
before any such ethics or legislation existed. In the *Nihon Shoki*, written in Chinese, a certain amount of ethical coloring was added, but
even so it remains basically the same as the *Kojiki*, a far cry from
the didactic histories of the continental historian.

The fact that the national histories were produced by the state on
the basis of popular traditions meant that in their fundamental approach to history, the state and the people had not parted company.
The *Kojiki*, for example, adopts for its accounts the "tale" form so
beloved of the ordinary Japanese, and this national history is in turn
the direct precursor of the prose romances which in later ages were
to mark the beginning of a purely Japanese literature.

This is surely a remarkable proof of how essentially of the people
—i.e. national—was the best in the culture which grew up in the
central city of ancient Japan. Moreover, since that tradition was
never to encounter any upheaval such as could destroy it utterly, it
persisted at the heart of the higher levels of culture achieved later
on in Japanese history.

5

The Heian period was the age in which the ancient cultural forms
were most distorted—if this is the right word—since the Kyoto
aristocracy at this time, in much the same way as the aristocracy of
the walled cities of other countries in ancient times, wallowed in its
own decadence within a completely isolated, urban atmosphere. In
Japan's case, however, the history and literature of the age were
themselves quite aware of the realities of their society, and the result of this awareness was a type of history and literature which was
similar in its approach to that of modern literature. The romances
and diaries which characterized the literature of the period were,

in their literary approach and artistic expression, so far removed from the literary forms and attitudes of the Six Dynasties on the Chinese mainland that it is hard to believe that they were the product of an age which was, in fact, influenced by the literature of China of that period. Likewise, the fondness of the age for reading the *Shih-chi* of Ssu-ma Chien may be attributed in part to the fact that of all the earlier Chinese histories, it was most free from the didactic approach to history usual in China. The histories in *kana* which first came into being in this period looked on history from the human standpoint, with something akin to the modern psychological approach. This is shown by the *Eiga Monogatari*, which is in a completely different class even from the *Kojiki* and *Nihon Shoki*. A typical sign of the desire to see history from all kinds of different angles is the method adopted, for example, in the *Ōkagami* and *Mizukagami*, where elderly men well versed in the affairs of the world are made to relate bygone events. Another method often found in later historical literature and essays is to have people with somewhat differing viewpoints discuss the subject together, the interesting thing here being that each viewpoint is admitted in its own right, with no attempt necessarily made to pass a final verdict on them. In historical works, facts are accepted as such without any attempt to pass moral judgments on them as was done on the continent. There are even some writers, such as the author of the *Mizukagami*, who consciously stress this point. This is not necessarily, as one might suspect, a result of a Buddhistic fatalism or of the feeling, widely held at the time, that the "Latter Day" of the Buddhist Law was at hand. "Since it is only natural," he says, "that with the Latter Day of the Law the teachings of the Buddha should lose their hold and society become degenerate, it is a mistake to lay down what is right and what is wrong. One should not deceive oneself into thinking that everything without exception is wicked." This is no fatalistic resignation, but a desire to see facts as they are.

It is a characteristic of the Japanese attitude toward history that

42

it tends to see it in terms of human psychology. This trait is apparent in the medieval military chronicles, which are history colored by the human emotions. Yet at the same time the Japanese approach to history also reveals another, diametrically opposed aspect, which is objective and descriptive. The official histories adopt this approach; their prefaces include such phrases as "to bequeath an example to posterity," or "to distinguish between good and evil, so as to provide a guide for reward and punishment," but this does not necessarily mean that the content is distorted for didactic purposes. Works such as the *Azuma Kagami* are, in fact, faithful reporting.

In short, although the Japanese approach history objectively they have two different ways of doing so. One is the "human" approach, the kind of objectivity seen in the romances; the other, and more purely objective approach, which sees facts simply as facts, is typified by the *Azuma Kagami*. Neither sees history as a source of moral [17] instruction.

This does not mean, however, that no moral values at all are sought in history. Value, in fact, is recognized in the objective truth of historical facts. It was this approach that, at the very dawn of history-making, made possible the *Kojiki*, a work which is free of any moral preconceptions. Unlike the history with which Confucius is said to have struck awe into the rebels of the day, which was a perversion of the facts through moral awareness, the Japanese presented historical truth as a means of correcting a distortion of the moral sense. The *Jinnō Shōtōki* of Kitabatake Chikafusa is generally regarded as the first work of this kind, but it merely happens to be the first work written with such a conscious intent; the same purpose was also present, unconsciously, in the histories of the Nara and Heian periods. The *Dai Nihon-shi* and *Nihon Gaishi* may have presented con- [18,19] scious moral statements along with their facts, but they were no different from other works in giving the truth about Japanese history precedence over ethical theory. On the continent, each succeeding dynasty, faced with the need to justify the establishment of its own

regime and condemn that of the previous dynasty, found itself obliged to deny any such thing as an absolute historical truth. In Japan's case, history plain and unvarnished was held, on the contrary, to be a guide in determining the correct moral course for the nation.

This attitude toward history has much in common with the realistic approach of Japanese literature. Both spring, in fact, from the same sources. In the history of Japanese literature, the realistic approach originates in the classical period. With the Middle Ages, the classical spirit began to be distorted, until eventually the *kogaku* of Tokugawa times called for a revival of classical spirit. As we have already seen, however, medievalism in Japan was not, as in Europe, a result of the control of a central, supra-national power such as the Church of Rome, but of domestic political changes, and thus was not so far removed from the classical tradition.

6

In contrast to the continental civilizations of Europe and Asia in ancient and medieval times, which were civilizations, rather, of the citadel state, ancient Japanese civilization had, as we have seen, a nationwide character which produced a uniquely Japanese classicism in history and literature. Modern civilization in the West was the result of a shift from the ancient and medieval "civilization of the state" to a "civilization of the people," but in Japan preparations along these lines had already been made in ancient and medieval times. In medieval times such preparations consisted, in every country alike, of the emergence of a bourgeoisie, but in the West, where this phenomenon was consequent on the development of the guild towns, the guild towns and the feudal barons were antagonistic, and cooperation between them was impossible. Thus the extension of the power of the bourgeoisie led to a decline in the power of the feudal lords and to a new national unity, which led in turn to eman-

cipation of the states from the power of the Roman Church and to the establishment of independent nations.

In Japan too, the process in principle followed the same course, though there was no Reformation leading to emancipation from a higher international authority. There were peculiar features, however, in the process of preparation for the modern state in Japanese medieval history. During the age of samurai rule in Japan, the feudal lords and the newly arising bourgeois class were not set at opposite poles, but enjoyed a relationship similar to that of the modern state and the bourgeois in the West. Foreign trade, which had declined toward the end of the Heian period, started up again under the government of the warrior clans, and showed particular development from the time of the Ashikaga shoguns on, when it was carried on 20 by the temples and townsfolk in cooperation for the benefit of the shogun's family's own pocket. Trade by private individuals was banned in order to protect the monopoly, but from the Heian period on it appears to have gone on in secret, despite the halt to official trade, and relations with Sung China in the Kamakura period were probably not confined, as one might think, to priestly exchanges. It is not clear what motive inspired Sanetomo's plan to cross to Sung 21 China, but the fact that he had such a large ship specially built is enough to suggest that the aims were not purely scholarly. The official ban on exchanges during the Hōjō era probably represented a 22 determination to close the country, even at the expense of the benefits accruing from exchanges, inspired by fear that the wave of Mongol aggression on the continent would inevitably lap at the shores of Japan—an expectation which was borne out by events. Then in the Ashikaga period, when the threat had disappeared, reaction brought in its wake trade with Ming China, both public and private, on a nationwide scale, and the age of the *wakō* ensued. 23

This occurred around the same time as the discovery of the New World in the West, and shows that the civilization of Japan was not lagging behind the rest of the world in enterprise. In fact, in the

45

relationship between the feudal state and the new bourgeoisie Japan was, if anything, one step ahead. Just as the Ashikaga government collaborated with ordinary citizens in foreign trade, so the feudal lords cooperated with the citizens in their respective districts, or provided the capital for the *wakō*, in an attempt to increase the national wealth through foreign trade. One family in particular, the Ōuchi, acquired a dominant position and became the wealthiest of all the feudal lords. None of them, however, was content simply to profit from license fees from the guild merchants as did the barons of Europe. In other words, although medieval society in Japan assumed the outward form of a military state, there were already signs of a trend toward a modern bourgeois society. Because of this, the fighting which ravaged the whole country in the subsequent Sengoku age did not lead to nationwide exhaustion; in fact, by cooperating with the trading merchants the feudal lords actually increased their wealth. Hideyoshi's expedition to Korea had the backing of that wealth, and in one sense might even be considered a deliberate device to exhaust it. The surprising lack of opposition from rivals encountered by the Tokugawas in their subsequent task of unifying the nation could be attributed in part to the effect of the Korean expedition in relieving the feudal lords of the surplus money that might have tempted them into action.

Whatever the case, the civilization of medieval Japan acquired in this way certain bourgeois characteristics which mitigated its otherwise exclusively military nature. The samurai were sprung from the powerful families of the provinces, which had lost contact with the culture and learning of the classical age. Even where they had originally come of imperial or Kyoto-aristocratic stock, they had become too countrified, after long years in the provinces, to keep up with the main tradition of culture. Yet even in the Kamakura period, when they relied almost exclusively on imitation of Kyoto culture, the warriors were inclined to view that culture as decadent —Minamoto no Sanetomo was even criticised by other samurai for

24

being too "Kyotofied" and the samurai inevitably began to branch off in search of their own culture as distinct from that of Kyoto. They were not completely successful in this, but by assimilating with the bourgeois culture below it, samurai culture was able in the natural course of events to evolve cultural forms to some extent different from, if not actually independent of, those of Kyoto.

The sole advisors to the warriors were the priests, who were responsible for everything, even including the substitution of the *renga* (linked verse) for the poetic pastimes of Kyoto, and of the Nō and its music for the courtly *bugaku* and its orchestra. These same priests, however, also associated with the townsmen, and cooperated with them in their overseas trade. From the time of the "Tenryū-ji ships" sent to trade with China in the Ashikaga period in order to earn money for the construction of the Tenryū-ji Temple, the priests had close connections with the merchant society. More accurately, it seems likely that the priests had been playing an intermediary role in trade ever since the opening of religious exchanges with Sung China, and that this merely encouraged the Ashikaga government to make use of the temples for trade purposes. Thus, the priests came to hold a similar position as cultural mentors in relation to the merchants as they did to the samurai. Their mediation thus created a cultural liaison—of which the tea ceremony was a good example—between the warriors and the merchants. At the tea ceremony, the samurai and merchants met on completely equal terms. Indeed, the merchant more often than not occupied a more honored place than the samurai—a sign of how the samurai had come to depend financially on the wealth of the merchant families.

In this way, the medieval civilization of Japan, at no time cut off from the classical culture by the political or religious control of other nations, similarly escaped from the alienation of religious and secular civilization that afflicted the West. In the forms they assumed, the samurai, priestly, and merchant cultures of medieval times were less conflicting than intermingled, giving the age a civilization with

47

a very special sensibility of its own, a sensibility quite different in nature from that of medieval European civilization.

7

The medieval sensibility in Japan was characterized by a comparative rejection of the excessive proliferation of detail, the "waste of sensibility" which marked the medieval civilization of Europe. Medieval civilization in Japan shared, it is true, the intensification of religious coloring in the culture as a whole which was seen in the West. However, religion at the time consisted principally of Zen Buddhism among the samurai, and of the Buddhism of the Nichiren and—still more widely—the Shin sects among the common people. All of these were free from any Scholastic-type tendencies in their teachings. I find it difficult to accept Okakura Tenshin's view that the esthetic sensibility of the samurai civilization should be attributed entirely to Zen, since I believe that this civilization had its roots still deeper, in the traditional Japanese sensibility as expressed in the classical civilization, though it is undeniable that the Buddhistic culture of the Middle Ages did have an influence on the cultural forms of the warrior age—even though in the direction of simplification rather than added complexity.

The reason why the warrior civilization did not lose contact with the uniquely Japanese sensibility of the classical culture is that, although the samurai since the Kamakura period had been seeking to evolve their own cultural style and thus bolster their own prestige by introducing a leavening of new civilization from Sung China, the spirit in which the imports were made was, as ever, essentially a product of the culture of Kyoto. This culture had from early times achieved a creative status of its own—to the extent that by the Heian period the aristocracy already found out-and-out imitation of continental culture as practiced by the aristocracy of the Nara period

48

quite impossible—and since the warrior class in Japan made no move, either politically or culturally, to displace Kyoto from its absolute position, the first step toward the creation of a samurai culture was, inevitably, the taking over of the Kyoto tradition. With this tradition as their starting-point, the samurai strove to branch off in new directions, yet they were unable to shake off the love of restraint which had been the essence of the classical civilization. The Ashikagas, for instance, are popularly supposed to have been brought low by their love of extravagance, yet the much-vaunted "lavishness" of their archite cture consists, in practice, of applying gold or silver foil to pavilion-style buildings so small that one might well bump one's head on the ceiling! The culture of the Momoyama period—the product of Japan's first accumulation of wealth, an accumulation achieved thanks to the complete unification of the country by Toyotomi Hideyoshi and to his mercantile policies—is generally supposed to have been a culture of a brilliance such as to shatter the traditional forms. Nonetheless, compared with the vast-ness and proliferation of detail apparent in the culture of the great military empires of both East and West, the operation of the taste for restraint is still very much in evidence. This is particularly true when one considers the tea ceremony which, since Ashikaga times, had come to represent the common sensibility of the warrior and merchant societies, and which, with the appearance of Sen no Rikyū in this period, manifested the love of restraint in its most character-istic form. Even the tea ceremony, of course, had its reverse side. The increased wealth of the warrior and merchant classes gave rise to a taste for rare utensils imported in the course of overseas trade. This led to a perversely exaggerated taste for the restrained, and to the paying of exorbitant prices for "rare pieces." In fact, the cult assumed such proportions that, from the time of Nobunaga and Hideyoshi on, bowls and other articles used in the tea ceremony came to be bestowed on individuals, much in the fashion of decora-tions, for worthy service in samurai society. In some ways, as this

27

49

shows, the tea ceremony developed the same inverted pretentiousness as was to lead the merchants of the Edo period to plate their
gold smoking-pipes with copper. Yet despite such excesses, the rejection of the exaggerated and the overdetailed proper to the tea
ceremony still survived in both the spirit and the form. The great
28,29 tea ceremony held by Hideyoshi at Kitano may have been somewhat
overdone in its scale, yet it contained no element of vulgar ''class''
display, being open to anyone, high or low, from anywhere in the
country. The quality in the tea ceremony of the samurai-aristocracy
and the merchants was established once and for all in this period.
At the same time, the love of restraint shown in the ceremony's
outward forms was carried to extremes; the tea ceremony room
became smaller and smaller, and the utensils used became more and
more humble in appearance.

Two terms often used to express the essence of the cultural outlook of medieval Japan are *wabi* and *sabi*. Much is made of their emphasis on a special type of restrained beauty, and especially on the—
in modern terminology—''assymetrical beauty'' which is its visible
manifestation and which Okakura Tenshin refers to as ''incomplete-
ness.'' Yet the true spirit of *sabi* and *wabi* lies less in a mechanical
''asymmetry'' than in the cultural restraint imposed on the vital
impulse. It is an ostensible return to a more primitive stage of civilization, based on the operation of the cultured sensibility in curbing
the instinctive desires, with their hankering after ever-fresh stimuli
in daily life. In appearance a putting-back of the clock of civilization
to primitive times, it is in fact a process of continuous spiritual refinement of primitive forms. In external appearance, the tea room
in the *sukiya* style is no more than a humble rustic cottage, yet in
fact the ''asymmetric'' or ''incomplete'' beauty of its architecture
represents a ''primitive'' form so extremely refined, an expression
so perfect of a particular sensibility, that not an inch could be added
to or subtracted from the dimensions of its pillars or its windows,
from the details of its plan or its elevation. It is the ''savage'' brought

to perfection by the civilized outlook. The display of beauty here serves, not to stimulate the senses, but to give the sensibility a new simplicity.

This love of restraint was, paradoxically, one aspect of that very Momoyama culture which has been compared to the culture of France under Louis XIV. Indeed, what are usually considered the "Momoyama" elements in the culture of the age of Hideyoshi were in fact merely the outward show, in the same way as the Buddhist culture of the Nara period; it is in the realms of *wabi* and *sabi* that the age is seen really "at home." It is a tradition of Japanese civilization that the glittering and the majestic should always be accompanied by its opposite, that a *Nihon Shoki* should always have its *Kojiki*.

8

In political terms, the establishment of the Tokugawa Shogunate meant the setting-up of a central authority of the ancient type which at the same time preserved the forms of the warrior state; yet in its culture the period advanced toward the stage of modernity. Ieyasu's use of Confucianism to curb the power of the temples had much in common with the freeing of government and culture from *30* the dominance of the church which was the first stage in the establishment of the modern state all over the world. The development of every single one of the medieval forms of the samurai culture was cut short, and the culture of the merchant class came to enjoy almost absolute sway. Despite the powerful backing of the daimyos, the various traditional arts were forced into the stagnancy of "establishment" art, and the arts of the merchant class arose to take their place.

In its essential nature, the civilization of the Tokugawa period would seem to manifest in its most thoroughgoing form that truly national quality which we have already seen as characterizing Japa-

nese culture. There can have been few cases, even among the modern
nations of the West, where a culture which first emerged from the
lower strata of society came to form, as it were, a pyramid with such
a broad base. It was, of course, an urban culture, yet it was not a
centralized culture focused in a single city, but had two great strongholds: the Kantō and Kansai areas, respectively. This is interesting
not only as showing how culture in Japan spread out into the provinces, but also as another sign of how truly Japanese culture belonged to the people themselves. One is justified in describing the
culture of the Tokugawa period as having emerged from below, or
as forming a broad-based pyramid, since the cultural backbone of
the nation at the time was the culture of the merchant class, which
had economic control of the nation, rather than that of the warrior
class, which had political control. The feudal samurai culture died,
in fact, just as the warriors brought their political organization to
its finest perfection. This was, as we have already seen, a result of
the gradual organization of the merchant class which had been getting under way ever since Ashikaga times—a process which was
already leading, in the period from the Ashikaga period on into the
Sengoku age, to the permeation of samurai society by merchant
culture.

The tea ceremony was a case in point. The priest Murata Shukō
31 is said to have taught Ashikaga Yoshimasa the style of tea ceremony
favored by the merchants, which arose in the trading port of Sakai,
and later writing on the tea ceremony quotes an account in the
32 *Nochikagami* which begins, "Nowadays something known as the tea
ceremony is performed among the common people, and there is a
monk called Shukō who is an adept . . . ." However, even before
this, in Kamakura times, the drinking of tea had become a popular
pastime, and there was a fashion in aristocratic society for contests
in which the participants, for prizes, attempted to guess the type of
tea they were drinking. Among the samurai, too, the tea ceremony
33 of the type held in a special room of a *shoin*-style residence was being

performed, and the way in which the samurai class now transferred
its preference from the aristocratic style of tea ceremony to the
merchant style was another sign that the cultural opposition of
classes was not a fundamental thing in Japan. The same was true of
the Nō drama, which was essentially the rustic *sarugaku* transformed   34
into art by the sensibility of the warrior age—and by the end of
the Sengoku period, moreover, the interest of the warrior class was
already being diverted to the *onna kabuki* which had sprung up in the   35
merchant cities. Even the Nō itself, that quintessence of the symbolic in art, had had to be accompanied, in the samurai culture, by
the *kyōgen* farces, which incorporated a popular element more typical of merchant culture. The dominance of the merchant culture,
in fact, was in no sense an overnight development of the Tokugawa
period.

Nevertheless, it was with the Tokugawa period that that dominance became absolute, and it was in this period that art in general
freed itself from the fetters of feudal patronage and became a free
occupation catering for the merchant class, which appropriated to
itself all the higher forms of culture. From around the Genroku era,
literature, painting, the theater, music—indeed, all the fine and
decorative arts without exception—came to develop in accordance
with merchant tastes, and were enjoyed by a cultural stratum
which included the very lowest levels of society.

The ukiyo-e (woodblock print) expressed the sensibility of its age
so thoroughly that it might well be called the first truly Japanese type
of picture, completely independent of the continental heritage. Its
vulgarity—or, if that term is misleading, its escape from the restrictions of classical elegance—sprang from the fact that it found its
audience in, and had its roots in the sensibility of, the class just
mentioned. The craftsmen who produced the ukiyo-e gave expression
to their own feelings, rather than those of some patron who had
commissioned the work. For this same reason, it took the form of a
woodblock print, which made it, as a work of art, as readily ac-

53

cessible physically to every segment of society as it already was spiritually. The appearance of a type of picture expressing the sensibility of the age at its best at such a low cost and in a form so readily accessible to the whole of society was something of which the most civilized country of Europe, with the widest dissemination of culture, could never boast. Nothing like it is known today, or is likely to be known again in the future.

9

Everything in the civilization of the Tokugawa period was truly "national" in this sense. The literary revival, having first occurred as a kind of neo-classicism, was unable at first to permeate all strata of society, but by the end of the same Genroku era there had emerged a popular literature which was to carry it down to the lower strata as well. Just as, in the Heian period, the creation of the *kana* syllabary had given rise to a purely Japanese type of literature potentially available to the whole nation as a substitute for the Chinese writings, inaccessible to ordinary people, which had hitherto constituted all of literature, so the Tokugawa-period renaissance evolved its own special means of disseminating literature by carrying the use of the *kana* syllabary to extremes. The popular novelettes *(sōshi)*, with their ties with medieval religion, gave way to a more modern literature freed from such preoccupations. Thus the *e-zōshi*, a kind of extension of the "picture-scroll" form using pictures accompanied by a text written entirely in *kana*, came into being and provided literature for the whole nation.

Yet even in this period, the traditional preference of Japanese culture for visual and aural media rather than the written word still persisted, and actually extended its scope. The Kabuki, a merchant-class art developed out of the early and artistically immature *onna-kabuki*, attained a fairly high artistic level at an even earlier date than

the popular literature. All kinds of ballads and recitations similarly improved on the forms existing since medieval times and became an organized part of people's lives. The recitation of works such as the *Heike Monogatari* and *Taiheiki*, with their martial themes, was re- 36,37 placed by forms such as the *jōruri*, *kōdan*, and *rakugo*, which had a 38–40 civilizing influence at all levels of society, shaping intellect, emotions, and sensibility to an extent scarcely possible through books alone. The same was true of music. We have already seen how Japanese music throughout the ages was not an art of the human voice or the sound of instruments as such, but a kind of program music with an explicit bearing on everyday life. In the same way, the music of this period, apart from a little instrumental music, consisted entirely of a refining through melody of the emotions of everyday life. In this respect, the music of the period revives the civilizing role played by the oral traditions in the age before the acquisition of a script. It was a process of civilizing through the intellect and, still more, through the sensibility. Moreover, this musical culture permeated the nation to the extent that scarcely any household where there were women lacked it entirely. Indeed, the feeling for music of the Japanese of the Tokugawa period was so developed that it proved too much for men of the modern period to carry on.

In its literary trends, too, the Tokugawa period looked back across the intervening Middle Ages directly to the Nara and Heian periods. The outlook and style of Saikaku's work link up with those 41 of the age of the *Kojiki*—or at least with the *Genji Monogatari*, which 42 itself looks back over an age of Chinese-style literature to the *Kojiki*. In this sense, though Saikaku's work may represent an exaggeration of the literary tradition existing from ancient times, it is in no sense a perversion of that tradition. Indeed, when *Genji* was adapted for a Tokugawa-period audience, its "decadence" proved to have such relevance for contemporary society that it offended the authorities of the day. This could only happen because of the way in which, in Japanese literary history, the ancient age looks forward to the mod-

ern and the modern back to the ancient, and is another proof that ancient Japanese civilization is present in essence at the roots of all subsequent Japanese civilization.

Yet in another sense, this merely shows how—in cultural matters as in their approach to history—the Japanese try to keep in touch with the actualities of the age. The consciousness of the more corrupt aspects of actuality shown in the revived popular interest in *Genji* is a fundamental prerequisite of a true awareness of society in its members' everyday lives, a prerequisite which from earliest times the Japanese were careful to fulfill. Of course, where official cultural policy is concerned, too obvious a public flaunting of this awareness must be checked, since it tends to induce not awareness in the good sense, but a wallowing in decadence for its own sake. However, a society devoid of all such self-knowledge, far from being more healthy, is a society with a deep-rooted malady. The Japanese had this self-awareness to a considerable degree even in ancient times, at a stage when it is usually supposed to be immature, which is precisely what makes ancient Japanese literature so prophetic of modern literature, in which that consciousness is so developed.

To turn now to poetry, the *waka* (Japanese verse in lines of five and seven syllables) had been the literary form of the whole nation only in ancient times; by the Heian period its formalization at the hands of the aristocrats had begun to put it outside the scope of the people as a whole. Even so, the form remained the rhythmical speech, as it were, of every class of society even in the warrior age, and an ignorance of it was considered a disgrace among the samurai.

In practice, however, the *waka* had become too encumbered with formal aristocratic restrictions to serve as a satisfactory form for the merchant culture. The first result was the evolution of the *renga* (linked-verse) which involved the linking together of *waka* written in a freer language than before, and when the form of the *renga* in turn became too complex and difficult as a result of conventions imposed by what amounted to a guild of *renga* makers, there emerged

from it the drastically simplified *hokku* form, which consisted of the first seventeen syllables of the *renga* form treated as an independent verse. This became the most widespread form of merchant-class literature, restoring to literature once more its traditional non-exclusive, nationwide character.

Until the time of Matsunaga Teitoku the *haiku*—as the *hokku* in its *43* fully independent form came to be known—concentrated on a characteristic kind of wit and humor, seeking to provide a readily understandable literature for the common people, reflecting their own speech and feelings, as a counter to the formal and expressive aristocratization of the *waka*. Yet even here it is characteristic of Japanese culture that the development of this form of literature should have proceeded with the active encouragement of that very aristocratic society against which it was a reaction. For example, the Emperor Gomizunoo, who was well versed in the classics and no mean *44* *waka* poet, personally composed *haiku* such as the following: "Leaping over the stream by a paddy field to pick the green leaves." *45* This kind of thing obviously helped increase the nationwide popularity of the *haiku*. In most cases, what is meant by a "national civilization" is the civilization of either the upper or lower—usually the upper—section of society. That the traditional civilization of Japan was not so but, literally, a civilization of the whole people was an outcome of the universally shared cultural sensibility of which this is an example.

In time, the *haiku* became associated with the cult of *wabi* and *sabi* already mentioned above, which formed another aspect of merchant culture. The result was the style of the great *haiku* master Bashō and *46* his followers. In doing so, it became the property of a class with a cultural sensibility somewhat more highly developed than the average, and began to smack somewhat of literary dilettantism. Yet, at the same time, it still remained the literature of the merchants themselves; indeed, the more conventional type of *haiku*, which remained at a lower literary level than this new type, came to be

57

practiced more widely than ever, and amateur poets were a penny a dozen. The elders of the various districts of towns such as Edo and Osaka were usually the judges at local *haiku* contests.

That the same form should have been made the vehicle for a still more plebeian outlook, producing *kyōku, senryū* and the like, is a sure sign of the insistence of the Japanese on keeping their civilization nationwide. Such low-level, peripheral cultural phenomena as these are, in fact, peculiarly important to any understanding of Japanese civilization. Western newspapers may have their columns of jokes and anecdotes, but is there any country of the West where ordinary people have inscribed literary forms such as *kyōku, senryū,* and *jiguchi* on lanterns and hung them about the place at their local town or village festivals? Or where a *haiku* written by a local resident could be framed and hung in the place of honor over the entrance to the local shrine? I doubt if such things could happen in other countries, even those with quite highly developed civilizations. They could only happen somewhere like Japan where the civilization is a truly national one. The "literature" in question here may be of a very low order, but rather than despise it for that, should one not despise the absence, in other towns and villages, of *any* literature, whatever the level?

Japanese civilization since the Meiji era has raised countless new, vastly complex questions to test the modern Japanese. If they are to deal with them successfully, the vital need is a strict appreciation of the traditional characteristics of Japanese civilization, and a conscious determination to preserve its virtues and remedy its shortcomings. Some aspects of this question will be dealt with in the following chapter.

III TRADITIONAL CULTURE AND
MODERN CULTURE

I

Whichever period of Japanese history one cares to examine, "traditional" culture and "modern" culture are invariably found to be flourishing side by side: in an extremely "modern" period, something extraordinarily "traditional" always begins to revive. By "modern" here is meant, of course, not "modernistic" but the typical products of a particular age, or of the influence of foreign civilizations in that age. Thus the Buddhist architecture of the Nara period represents the "modern" culture of that period. So did the writings in Chinese which formed the literature of the same period, and in the same way the Western-type literature of the Meiji period was "modern" in relation to its time.

It is usually as a reaction to such influences from alien civilizations that the "traditional" arises once more, yet in Japan's case the two do not alternate with each other, but go hand in hand in one and the same period. This was so even in the time of Prince Shōtoku, *48* that most "modern" of ages. Despite his reputation for idolizing things foreign, the Prince himself was the first to plan the compilation of a national history, and the author of the celebrated document addressed by "the Emperor of the Land of the Rising Sun" to the "Emperor of the Land of the Setting Sun." In the same way, the second year of the Meiji era (1869), when Japan was so busy taking over foreign systems, saw the establishment of an official bureau for the compilation of national histories, and by around 1877 it had produced various kinds of works. Even such individual "worshipers"

59

of things foreign as Fukuzawa Yukichi and Mori Arinori were both notable—in a new sense—for their respect for the traditional.

This collaboration between modern and traditional is particularly conspicuous in the field of literature. The *Tale of Genji*, produced in an age when literature in Chinese was considered to be the only literature, was doubtless extremely "modern," yet the literary outlook it embodied looked back, as we have already seen, beyond the contemporary preoccupation with Chinese learning to the oral literature of ancient times. The first truly Japanese literature was a developed form of the *monogatari* (prose romance) peculiar to Japan —the form taken by oral literature of the age before the existence of a system of writing—and all subsequent literature showed the influence of this earliest form, the "new literature" of each age in turn adopting a "classical" ("pseudo-archaic") style. The military chronicles of medieval times, as might be expected of literature written by monks, showed a greater influence from Chinese-style writings, but the literary spirit they embodied was not continental, the deeds of their heroes being recounted, rather, in the manner of the native *monogatari* and in terms of Japanese emotions. The classical trend is even more marked in the works of men of culture such as
49,50 Yoshida Kenkō and Kamo Chōmei. The literary revival of the Tokugawa period similarly had a strongly marked neoclassical flavor, particularly where the structure of its sentences was concerned. Saikaku's work owed its influence—which extended even to the new literature of the Meiji period—to the fact that it was a kind of summing-up of the same trend.

In the Meiji era, under the influence of Western literature, there was much talk of making a clean sweep of the style of the popular prose novels of the late Tokugawa period, yet as late as the 1880's
51 works such as Tsubouchi Shōyō's *Shosei Katagi* still had not shaken off
52 their influence completely. Even Futabatei Shimei's *Ukigumo* is strongly influenced by Tokugawa literature, giving the impression of using a traditional form as a vehicle for Western-style literary ideas. It is

true, of course, that the popular tales of the late Tokugawa period were already remarkably "modern" in both content and form, yet the fact remains that the modes of expression peculiar to the Tokugawa period were no longer really suitable for expressing the culture of the Meiji era, and it is all the more interesting, therefore, that in its modes of expression the new literature which the first students of foreign literature attempted to create in Japan should have been so influenced by them.

In the early 1890's, literature showed a still stronger tendency to revert in its manner to the traditional literature of old Japan. This time, models were found still earlier—in Saikaku of the mid-Tokugawa period, in the medieval chronicles, or even in the literature of the Heian period—rather than in the literature of the late Tokugawa period. Novels even appeared in a pseudo-archaic style known as *gabuntai* ("elegant style"), and Mori Ōgai actually translated 53 foreign literature into this style. The writers who tried to establish new forms of expression for Meiji literature found themselves obliged, in fact, to turn for a while to a rather crude pseudo-archaic style inspired by the classics. Subsequently, Japanese literature made great strides, and evolved modes of expression that can justly be called modern, but most of the great figures of this modern literature were either direct students, or at least lovers of, the classics.

2

This longstanding tendency of the Japanese to combine in one age, or in one individual, both the traditional and the modern is a trait of Japanese civilization which should perhaps be welcomed as a model for the national culture as a whole. If the ability to live in harmony with others without losing his own individuality is the most desirable quality for the individual in society, then surely the most desirable civilization is that which demonstrates the same capacity.

In order to achieve this, however, it is vitally necessary to be ready not merely to advance in the direction of the new, internationally-oriented culture, but also to ensure the true continuance of the old "traditional" culture. The "tradition" in question must not stop at preserving unchanged what is old, as in a museum—though this is important, too—but must seek to embody in the cultural forms of a new age the same Japanese sensibility as gave birth to things traditional.

Different ages in Japan each gave rise to different cultural forms. These were not isolated cultures, however, but were given continuity by a consistent sensibility inherited by society and the nation as a whole. The cultural outlook of a particular nation gradually evolves and develops through contact with other civilizations, what distinguishes the process from mere aping of others being the fact that the development is backed up throughout by the special nature —the uniqueness—of the national sensibility. To take an example from the history of architecture, the first Japanese imitations of con-

54 tinental buildings—for instance, the Hōryū-ji Temple—displayed, we are told, a sensibility superior in some ways to that shown in the originals. In short, the Japanese of the day already had a highly developed cultural sense which could contribute something extra to the foreign prototypes. For the same reason, it was also possible for buildings displaying a sensibility utterly different from that of the continental prototypes to appear in Japan at the same period. The

55 *shinden-zukuri* style of architecture which first emerged around this time, though its layout was suggested by continental architecture, was in artistic spirit purely Japanese. That same spirit is still carried on in the Japanese dwelling of today.

Every sphere of Japanese culture in every age reveals signs of the taking over of foreign forms. However, though the Nō may have been influenced by the drama of Yüan China, what is still more certain is that within Japanese civilization it is given a new, unique character. However much the work of Murasaki Shikibu or of

Saikaku may have been influenced by literature in Chinese, the literary sensibility they display justifies one in speaking of the independence of Japanese literature, just as surely as Shintō shrine architecture and the *shinden-zukuri* style of residential architecture bear witness to the independence of Japanese architecture.

This ability of "modern" Japanese culture in every age to produce new, genuinely native forms is a result of the uninterrupted maintenance of the Japanese sensibility, particularly in the life of the individual. The aristocrats of the Nara and Heian periods, though following the continental manner in their temples, stubbornly based their dwellings on their own, quite different artistic taste, and a similar approach can be detected in Japanese life in every age. No parallel, for example, could be found in other countries for the existence in Japan today, side by side and for the use of the Japanese themselves, of both Japanese-style and foreign-style restaurants. In the Japanese, the desires to chase after foreign cultures and to cling to the traditional culture seem to exist in equal strength.

The cultural individuality of the Japanese resides in the spirit rather than in outward forms, and is therefore not always apparent to those—particularly those from other countries—who do not share the same sensibility. It is for this reason that foreigners fail to distinguish between genuine objects of Japanese art and the souvenir-type objects on sale in harbor towns—or even prefer the latter to the former! Should the hitherto-maintained continuity of sensibility be interrupted, the Japanese themselves would fall into the same insensitivity. They would doubtless give free rein to the desire to chase after things foreign and abandon their instinctive clinging to the traditional, producing a new culture displaying no individual sensibility of its own. Once this happened, no resurgence of the "traditional" could lead to anything more than a superficial imitation of old things, without the dynamic cultural creativity needed to embody the traditional sensibility in new, imported forms. Worst of all, it would lead to the unthinking imitation

of things in old, traditional forms but without the truly Japanese spirit. An actual case in point is the vulgar predeliction of the larger restaurants nowadays for buildings in a degenerate "Momoyama" style more reminiscent of a "Japanese room" in some foreign hotel.

This kind of thing is, indeed, already to be found in every sphere of modern Japanese culture. It is found in the political and academic spheres, and in all other fields of culture there is a similar fashion for the mechanical imitation, not only of new forms from abroad, but of the traditional native forms also. When the Japanese lose touch with their traditional sensibility and merely imitate what is old, it is no wonder that they should fall for the same "Oriental" exoticism as foreigners. Nor is the trouble confined to restaurants and cafés; it affects every aspect of culture and the social system.

If the traditional sensibility is to be understood, felt, and preserved in its pure form, it must be respected and encouraged in every field of daily life—in everything that meets the eye and affects the mind, whether in the school, the home, or society at large, whether in education, the arts, or the world of entertainment. Literature and the fine and applied arts are particularly fundamental forces in fostering and preserving such a sensibility, not only within their own spheres but in everyday life as a whole. The traditional sensibility of the Japanese is stamped with the mark of the natural, political, and social factors that gave it birth, and has been nourished by varied international influences, so that it is in no sense unsuited to Japan's needs in the modern world of today. Although the experience of the Japanese in applying a cultural sensibility already quite highly developed to the acclimatization of things Chinese can be paralleled in the experience of the Chinese and Greeks with the cultures of India and Central Asia, in Japan's case the native sensibility was not only maintained as a national tradition but also differed greatly in quality from that of the continent. The Japanese and continental systems of government were so fundamentally dif-

ferent that they created a complete difference of atmosphere between the political sensibilities of the two sides.

In practice today, the traditional refinement of sensibility tends
to be preserved as though in a museum, with no means of development as a living force in society and the nation as a whole. In every
period of Japanese history so far, Japan has succeeded in using elements from other countries in order to create something at once new
and in accord with the traditional sensibility. In the Heian period,
the prose romances were born under the influence of the Chinese
script. In the time of the Ashikagas, the Nō was born under the
influence of the drama of Yüan China, and the tea ceremony under
the influence of Zen. In the Tokugawa period, again, Chinese literature was to assist at the birth of the characteristic literature of the
Genroku era and later, and the Chinese theater at the birth of the
Kabuki. One cannot but wonder whether the Japanese of the present
and future age will be able to live up to the example set by their
predecessors in this respect.

IV ON JAPANESE CIVILIZATION

I

The idea is comparatively common among foreigners and Japanese alike that since Japanese civilization inherited so much from those of China and Korea, Japanese culture is therefore an offspring of Chinese culture, and that the Japanese are a race of skillful imitators with little real creativity. There are others, such as W. G. Aston, author of *A History of Japanese Literature*, who agree that the Japanese allowed themselves to be guided by China to an excessive extent, but hold that they were neither content with mere imitation nor deficient in creativity.

To say that Japanese civilization is inherited from the civilization of the continent does not, in fact, mean that it has no character of its own. Whatever the country, its civilization is invariably part of a larger cultural heritage. Without the contact, fusion, inheritance, and transmission of various different cultures, civilization would undergo no development. That the civilization of a country should have its own distinguishing characteristics does not mean that it has not derived from the civilization of another country or countries, but rather that one and the same cultural tradition has undergone certain special transformations in that country. One could not call the countries of Europe imitative, or deny them creative originality, simply because they have inherited the civilizations of Greece and Rome.

Right from prehistoric times Japan enjoyed international relations in the modern sense—i.e., peaceful economic exchanges—with the

countries of the Korean peninsula. The conquest of one of those kingdoms by the Empress Jingū at the beginning of the third century A.D. was only undertaken because that kingdom was a threat to the Kyūshū area of Japan, and was aimed, in a sense, at the restoration of peaceful exchanges. The first mention in recorded history of peaceful relations with foreign countries occurs at the beginning of the first century B.C. Moreover, it concerns a request for permission to return home made by a mission from a kingdom of the Korean peninsula, so that it seems certain that peaceful exchanges with other countries had been going on from considerably before this. It was about the same time that Japan began direct exchanges with Han China. Around the beginning of the third century, large numbers of specialists and workmen in the fields of crafts and civil engineering began to come to Japan from the continent for the first time in history; it is said that inhabitants from 127 districts of one country of the peninsula became naturalized Japanese on a single occasion, and there must have been a considerable amount of immigration both before and after this as well. Moreover, the Japanese government in ancient times officially recognized hereditary membership of occupational "guilds" among those engaged in particular industries in the various districts, and surnames were bestowed on each of these guilds. Craftsmen from the continent who had become naturalized Japanese were given surnames in just the same way, and were apportioned among the different districts. There is a striking similarity to the methods of a modern civilized state in the way these foreign specialists were not kept simply to cater for the extravagant tastes of the aristocracy in the capital, but were sent out to help develop the industry of the country as a whole. Around the middle of the fifth century, the number of silk weavers among these workers of foreign descent was 20,000, and in the sixth century they accounted for 7,500 households. It is obvious just how much the beginnings of industry in Japan owed to foreigners, and it follows naturally that

68

ILLUSTRATION FROM "THE GENJI
MONOGATARI SCROLL," EARLY
TWELFTH CENTURY

A PORTION OF THE TEXT FROM "THE
GENJI MONOGATARI SCROLL"

KABUKI DANCE BEING PERFORMED AT SHIJŌGAWARA
(KYOTO), FROM THE SCREEN PAINTING "SCENES WITH-
IN AND WITHOUT THE CAPITAL," EARLY SEVENTEENTH
CENTURY

SCENE FROM THE NŌ PLAY "HANJO"

"DUSK AT SHINAGAWA," A WOODBLOCK PRINT (UKIYO-
E) BY KIYONAGA, EIGHTEENTH CENTURY

HIMEJI CASTLE, BUILT IN THE EARLY
SEVENTEENTH CENTURY

ILLUSTRATION FROM "THE HEIJI
MONOGATARI SCROLL," EARLY
THIRTEENTH CENTURY

GARDEN OF THE SAMBŌ-IN (KYOTO),
LATE SIXTEENTH CENTURY

IZUMO SHRINE, ORIGINALLY BUILT PRIOR TO 700 À.D.
AND LAST REBUILT IN 1744, ILLUSTRATES FEATURES OF
VARIOUS ARCHITECTURAL STYLES

ARMOR, THIRTEENTH
OR FOURTEENTH CEN-
TURY

DECORATIVE SWORD WITH MOTHER-
OF-PEARL WORK ON SCABBARD

many of the forms taken by ancient Japanese culture also had their origin in foreign cultures.

The same was true in the fields of learning and religion. The official histories record that scholars from the Korean peninsula brought works written in Chinese to Japan at the end of the third century, but since foreigners had been settling in Japan from earlier than this and a Japanese mission had actually been sent to the Han Empire at the beginning of the second century, it seems almost certain that Chinese documents and writing had reached Japan even before this date.

The enlightened outlook which the Japanese of ancient times displayed is clearly suggested by the account in the national history already mentioned above telling how the court, at the time of the first visits to Japan by Buddhist priests around the middle of the sixth century, allowed free discussion among the courtiers on the pros and cons of introducing a foreign religion into a country which already had its own native religion. The high level achieved by the civilization of the Nara and Heian periods—from the beginning of the seventh century until the latter half of the twelfth century— compared with other civilizations at the same period, was due to the conscious and enlightened efforts made by Japan to promote exchanges with other countries from the first and second centuries A.D. onward.

The large population of *hambetsu*—i.e., persons with names of Chinese origin, descendants of foreign immigrants—among the Japanese people in ancient times represented a peaceful, industrial immigration such as that seen in America in modern times, and not an additional population gained by conquest as in the ancient empires.

With this kind of history, it is no wonder that Japanese culture should include an enormous number of elements of foreign origin. Yet, as we have already seen, this does not make it an imitative cul-

ture. The taking-over of the civilization of the continent was no
more than an obvious shortcut toward the development by Japan
of a civilization of its own, the kind of taking-over which is necessary
if any people is to have its own culture. The question, rather, is the
way in which Japan imposed its own characteristic flavor on what it
had inherited. The same problem faced Japan in ancient times as
today. In ancient times Japan found itself faced with the task of forging a new civilization for itself by taking over the civilization of the
Oriental mainland, and modern Japan had to do the same with
the civilization of the West.

2

Those who stress the foreign origins of Japanese culture are coun-
56 tered by others who stress the "pure Japan." In particular, the
latter include many who point to the unique quality of the national
religious beliefs, or of the national ethical outlook. These are frequently people of a conservative bent who tend to boycott foreign
culture and oppose things progressive, but there is a certain truth in
their views nevertheless. While the Japanese, in ancient and modern
times alike, have always been extremely susceptible to the influence
of foreign culture, and extremely progressive in their willingness
to adopt it themselves, another side of them has always clung ob-
stinately to the traditional Japanese things. Not only do both sides
exist at the same period in the same country, but they not infrequently exist simultaneously in the same individual as well.

Any number of examples could be given, but I will content my-
self here with one or two of the most obvious. To take religion
first, it is usual in most countries for the native religion to disappear
by imperceptible degrees following the arrival of an international
religion. Yet in Japan the national religion was not abandoned when
Buddhism was first introduced, nor even later, when almost the

whole population had become practicing Buddhists. The house of a Buddhist believer invariably contained—in addition to the family Buddhist altar though in a different room—a miniature shrine dedicated to the native Shintō gods. Even today such houses are common, but even where there are no domestic shrines the Buddhist continues, as in the past, to combine his faith with the native Shintoism. Even adherents of the Shin sect of Buddhism and of Christianity—whose doctrines do not permit worship outside their own religions —still continue in practice to pay their respects at the Shintō shrines. This traditional outlook of the Japanese has persisted without the slightest change from the time of the introduction of Buddhism, fourteen hundred years ago, right up to the present, and can find few parallels in other countries.

The same kind of thing is true of architecture also. The Japanese style of residential architecture, though taking a number of hints from continental architecture in its layout, was utterly different from it in basic spirit. Here again the Japanese showed the same willingness to take over the foreign combined with a reluctance to abandon the native. This same attitude persists today; although public buildings, shops, and so on in the large towns are entirely Western in their architecture, the ordinary home still follows the traditional Japanese style of the past thousand years.

In matters of clothing, food, and entertainment as well, the Japanese have not taken over things foreign simply for their novelty, but have made them into an integral part of their own way of life; yet at the same time, they have not abandoned their own, unique things. Nor is this refusal to cast aside the traditional by any means confined to things spiritual. In the things most intimately connected with their everyday lives—in their clothing, for example, which includes both Japanese and foreign dress—they retain the traditional Japanese forms alongside the newly-adopted foreign forms, according equality of opportunity to both. They continue this even though they know that such a dual way of life is uneconomical.

This tendency of the Japanese to combine a broad-minded international quality with a stubborn taste for things Japanese derives
from their cultural dependence since ancient times on peaceful exchanges with foreign countries. Japan did not acquire cosmopolitan
contacts for the first time with the arrival of Perry at the end of the
Edo period. From the time of the Tokugawa Shogunate's edict clos-
ing the country—dictated by the view that Catholic missionary
activities were intended as a preliminary to territorial aggression
against Japan—the nation embarked on a period of prosperous isolation. Eventually the nation's finances, which had at first been eked
out with the aid of foreign trade, came to rely solely on domestic
agriculture; as a result, they rapidly fell into dire straits which in
time led to the collapse of the feudal system itself. However, even
during their period of seclusion, contact with China and Holland
was permitted on a small scale, and despite the few real chances for
contact this afforded, the Japanese continued ardent efforts to assimilate foreign culture just as their ancestors had done before them.
They succeeded in grasping, however imperfectly, at least the general outlines of modern history, political systems, ideas, science,
and so on, laying thereby the foundations necessary for the Meiji
Restoration.

The "Charter Oath," embodied in an imperial rescript at the
time of the Meiji emperor's ascension to the throne and said to
show the influence of modern ideas, is an expression of modern
Western thought as interpreted by the Japanese of the late Tokugawa period. At the same time, it is also an expression of traditional
Japanese ideas. The Japanese nation had had the experience of adopting a system of higher civilization from the continent in almost the
same spirit and with almost the same approach twelve hundred years
previously, and had carried through political reforms on that basis,
so that the outlook that informed the Meiji Restoration was in a
sense a very old, traditionally Japanese one.

Alongside the international qualities thus demonstrated, the Japa-

nese, in much the same way as the modern nations in the West, showed a strongly individual nationalist psychology as well, and they naturally possessed a unique national culture of their own. It is characteristic of the modern age that the development of world communications has centered on nations with strong national individualities, but a full thousand years ago Japan already bore some of the marks of the modern state as a unit in international relations, in that it combined a strongly international quality with a strong nationalist individuality. Any attempt to understand the character of Japanese civilization must be based on an understanding of this special quality of the Japanese state.

The fact that the greater part of Japan's cultural heritage, both tangible and intangible, is derived from the continent is a result of the cultural intercourse with other nations in which the Japanese engaged consciously from an early date. Unlike the situation in other ancient nations of both East and West, cultural intermingling did not occur as a fortuitous outcome of conquest, but through a conscious taking-over of foreign culture, much as a modern state might do. Nor was it the result of the emergence of a particular ruler at a particular period, as happened with Peter the Great in Russia, but of an enthusiasm for foreign culture surpassing that of Peter the Great which existed throughout the whole nation, from the emperor down to the common people, in every age.

These modern aspects of the Japanese state, with which the formation of ancient Japanese civilization was so inseparably bound up, have survived intact to the present day. In fact, one could claim that almost the whole of Japan's cultural heritage is characterized by this fusion of the international and the national.

3

It is difficult, even for the Japanese themselves, to grasp the essential

characteristics of Japanese civilization, and it may help to try comparing it with the civilizations of the West. A resemblance, for example, can be found between the way the civilization of China was taken over by Japan and the taking-over of the civilization of the ancient empire-states by a small tribal nation such as the Greeks. Ancient Japanese civilization is, in fact, frequently compared with that of Greece, but the resemblances between the two are confined to their having taken the characteristics common to all imperial civilizations in ancient times—the vastness, the crudeness, the complexity, and the attention to detail—and produced a miniature perfection, elegant, delicate, and comparatively uncomplicated. In Japan's case this was partly a result of the geographical, climatic, and other natural factors prevailing in Japan, but it was determined to a still greater extent by the nature and forms of the Japanese state and society, and by their relations with other countries.

If one examines the characteristics of Japanese culture from this angle, the first striking fact to emerge is that although Japanese culture derives from that of the continent, it has transformed it into something essentially different. In Japan, cultural forms which had their origins on the mainland become completely different in spirit. Although this is true of culture in all its different aspects, we must here confine ourselves to two or three examples from literature.

Aston's conclusion that the Japanese, while taking over the civilization of other nations, had evolved something original of their own was probably derived from his study of Japanese literature. The history of Japanese literature does, indeed, illustrate extraordinarily clearly the essential characteristics of Japanese civilization. It is only normal, of course, that the preoccupations of a literature should reveal the national character, but in the case of Japanese literature the history of its birth and development bears witness to the attitude and methods on which the Japanese built up the whole of their civilization.

As we have already seen, scholars were first brought to the court

from the continent around the third century A.D. From then on, cultural policy involved the wholesale importation of continental civilization, and the instilling of continental scholarship into the aristocracy and bureaucracy, using exclusively teachers from abroad, or their descendants. Scholars, physicians, and other specialists were invited from the continent on many occasions, though from the sixth century on, large numbers of Japanese students were also sent to study in China. Thus by around the middle of the fourth century a university modelled on T'ang lines had been set up in the capital, and others established at various points in the provinces as well. Many universities were also set up privately by priests, aristocrats, and others. Since a native script and native scholarship had not yet emerged, education at these universities consisted, of course, exclusively of Chinese learning, while the schools run by the priests taught Buddhism. Although such schools catered in practice for the sons of the aristocracy and the bureaucrats, in theory at least ordinary citizens could gain admission through examination. The schools were for men only, but there was a special system for training women physicians which actually produced women doctors of medicine. Many women at court and among the aristocracy were well-versed in the Chinese script; thus an empress could produce creditable Chinese prose, and an imperial princess excellent Chinese verse. In short, the women of the upper class were given a grounding in Chinese learning not inferior to that of men, a fact which was to help in the development by women, from the tenth on into the twelfth century, of a purely Japanese literature.

This means that for a long period, beginning in the second century, the Japanese were being given an exclusively Chinese-style education, and "literature" in the same period similarly meant Chinese literature. Yet in the long run the Japanese were not content to submit entirely to the sway of foreign culture, and were to evolve a purely Japanese literature of their own. The most elementary stage in this task was the evolution of a method of recording the

Japanese language by borrowing the sound or sense of the Chinese ideographs. The *Manyōshū* uses this method, setting down the sounds of purely Japanese verse in Chinese ideographs, while the *Kojiki*, Japan's first official history compiled at the court, (712), uses a mixture of this method and *kambun*, i.e., Chinese-style prose intended to be read as a kind of quasi-Japanese by reversing the order of the characters and supplying Japanese readings, particles, and so on. This method was to lead to the invention of a phonetic script based on Chinese ideographs. Priests who had been to China and had studied phonetics there devised a syllabary for representing the sounds of the Japanese tongue which is still in use today. It is based on the natural structure of the language, and consists of an orderly list of fifty sounds represented by abbreviated versions of selected Chinese characters. This *kana* syllabary was probably invented around the ninth century, but it did not come into general use until around the tenth century, and even then chiefly among women. As late as the twelfth century, men still considered it a disgrace to use Japanese written in *kana*.

However, the refusal of the Japanese to submit entirely to the continental-style script and literature was implicit in the very beginnings of the introduction of Chinese learning. The scholars of the countries of medieval Europe continued, parrot-like, to speak Latin and to read Latin in the same fashion as the Romans themselves for centuries after their first conquest by the Romans, but the Japanese had their own way of reading Chinese from the very outset. In many cases not only the verbs but the nouns as well were read, according to their meaning, with Japanese readings, and the words themselves were juggled to permit reading in a Japanese order. A parallel could perhaps be found in the way Greek and Roman proper names are pronounced in the local fashion in the countries of Europe, but there is no case of such a thoroughgoing making-over of a language as took place in Japan. The recitation of Chinese verses converted by this method into a kind of Japanese was a favorite pastime of the

aristocrats of the Heian period. I do not know whether any other nation has ever read foreign literature in this fashion, but nothing could show better how determinedly the Japanese of ancient times clung to the things of their own nation. Even today, the Japanese still deal with Chinese literature in the same fashion (an exception is the case of the Buddhist sutras, which are read by the priests in an approximation to the ancient Chinese pronunciations, though even here this method is not universal).

Such being the approach of the Japanese, it is not surprising to find that the purely Japanese literature written in the tenth century is fundamentally different from Chinese literature in both the sensibility and the sentiments it expresses. So marked, in fact, was the independence of manner characterizing the first purely Japanese literature that it seems certain to have constituted one of the factors which convinced Aston of the originality of the Japanese.

What is still more astonishing is that this Japanese literature should have been born, like man himself, of woman—a fact at back of which lies an important truth about the nature of education in ancient Japan.

Not only before the introduction of Chinese literature but for a long period after, the Japanese were educated chiefly via the oral traditions. The extreme delay in evolving a native script meant that education had to continue to rely on speech even after the awareness of its importance was comparatively highly developed. The traditions consisted largely of historical legends or verse, which were transmitted in a kind of rhythmical language, and it seems likely that they were generally current, since by the time that the introduction of Chinese characters had made possible the recording of these legends and verses, they included verses from every social class and from even quite outlying areas. Exchanges of verses were common among the general public in Japan from very ancient times; thus the *Manyōshū* records many exchanges of verse which took place between aristocrats in the town and maidens in farming or fishing villages.

Again, at the time when reserve troops were summoned from all over Kyūshū to prepare for possible invasion from the Korean peninsula, poems written by the soldiers were collected by the court. They contain a certain admixture of dialect, but they are, nevertheless, a witness to the extent to which the culture of the capital had spread to the outlying districts.

The prevalence of education at a time when writing was not yet available to the public at large is a sure sign that the oral culture of an earlier age continued to be practiced widely even after the introduction of the Chinese script. Indeed, with the increasing popularity of that script, oral education came to be practiced among even lower classes of society. At the beginning of the eighth century, when the court was proposing to draw up an official history of the nation for the first time, it searched among the general public for persons able to read, in the words of the old-style oral traditions, the ancient records written in Chinese characters. It found them, not among the aristocracy or the bureaucrats, but among low-ranking officials of the court. This shows how widely spread education by oral transmission was among ordinary people even before the establishment of any institutions of education. Nor was there such a vast difference between the upper and lower classes as regards the content of that education. Historical tales of the kind found in the *Kojiki*, for instance, were related by both alike; if it had not been so, it is unlikely that petty officials should have been able to read records of ancient legends where the aristocrats and scholars could not. From the time of the introduction of Chinese literature, the education of the upper class consisted chiefly of Chinese learning of the highest quality, and an enormous gap thus developed between the education of the upper and lower strata of society. Yet even so the traditional, verbally-transmitted education continued in society at large, and the ideas and emotions of the Japanese continued to be nurtured by it.

From ancient times the chief transmitters of that oral education were women. Education within the imperial family was trusted to

elderly women, and in all classes, high and low alike, it was the women who provided the oral education. Japanese women in ancient times were no less active than men, as is suggested by the fact that the only Japanese hero to conquer a foreign country in thousands of years was an empress—the Empress Jingū—but what is still more significant is that even the education of men, a matter affecting the culture of the nation as a whole, should have been carried out by women.

It was precisely because of the existence of such a tradition that the honor of developing the first truly Japanese literature went chiefly to women. It was for this reason, too, that in both form and content, true Japanese literature, at its first appearance, bypassed the tradition of several centuries of Chinese learning, and went back almost directly to the orally transmitted literature of ancient times. Not only was it utterly unlike the quasi-Chinese known as *kambun* in form, style, and treatment of its material, but it differed completely from Chinese literature in the literary sentiments expressed. This early Japanese literature took the form of *monogatari*. This word, often translated as "prose romance," originally meant simply "something told or related," and is in itself a hint that the first Japanese literature was a revival of the old literature transmitted by word of mouth.

The women who opened up this new field of literature were all well versed in Chinese learning. Murasaki Shikibu, the author of the *Tale of Genji*, was renowned for her knowledge of the continental classics, and most other court ladies of the day had similar accomplishments. That these same women should have created a completely original Japanese literature is an example of how the Japanese are constantly trying to develop their own civilization in its own independent fashion, however much they may import from abroad.

79

4

It is interesting that the first Japanese literature, originating in the way it did, should at the same time have demonstrated so many of the characteristics of modern literature. It was naturalistic; it observed life directly; its descriptions were comparatively realistic; and it portrayed its characters with considerable psychological depth. The oldest story surviving today, *Taketori Monogatari* (probably written at the beginning of the tenth century; the author is unknown, but it seems it was not a woman) adapts a fanciful Indian tale about a princess born from a bamboo who is brought up by an old peasant and is sought in marriage by many young nobles, only to disappoint them all in the end by ascending to heaven. This simple story is used in order to expose the corruption of contemporary aristocratic society. The *Tale of Genji*, written at the beginning of the twelfth century, is said to have had no parallel among world literature of its day where either length or richness of content are concerned. A review of the work in *The Times* of London noted that in Arthur Waley's translation *Genji* read surprisingly like a modern novel. In its style, the literature of the period is uninfluenced by Chinese, being comparatively close to the spoken language. It describes men and society from a modern, humanistic point of view; it is satirical; and it abounds in wit and humor of a type that one associates, rather, with modern English literature.

This trend represents a transfer to literature of the freedom of comment on the world and people around them which the women of the day allowed themselves in the personal diaries they customarily kept, not intended for outside eyes. Even the *Eiga Monogatari*, a lengthy history written by a woman at the end of the twelfth century, abounds in descriptions and points of view more characteristic of a novel. The same literary approach is apparent even in the *Kojiki*, which, as we saw earlier, was compiled by recording ancient oral

traditions as they stood. The *Nihon Shoki,* another national history compiled at the court—though it is somewhat later and written in *kambun*—is strongly influenced by Han literature in its handling of the narrative and in its ethical approach. It was this which led Moto-ori Norinaga, one of the pioneers of the classical revival in Tokugawa Japan, to declare that a comparison of the *Kojiki* and *Nihon Shoki* clearly revealed the contrast between the purely Japanese outlook, psychology, and ethic and their Chinese counterparts. Japanese literature, as goes without saying, inherits the literary tendencies of the *Kojiki,* the oral literature of ancient times.

The same features that distinguish the earliest Japanese literature are detectable throughout the whole of subsequent literature up to the present day. Around the end of the twelfth century, the warrior class gained exclusive control of the country, and the literature of the period naturally reveals a preoccupation with war; yet despite the inevitable tendency to hero-worship, it is also leavened with humanistic ideas derived from Buddhism, and retains the emotionalism of the literature of the Heian period. It is a literature less of the pride of the conqueror than of sympathy for the vanquished. In this respect, the battle literature of the Japanese feudal period is greatly different in mood from the battle literature of the continent. In the same period there even appeared a type of literature which implicitly criticized these feudal bickerings. Typical of this literature are the *Tsurezuregusa* and the *Hōjōki.*   57

The *yōkyoku,* the libretti of the Nō drama of medieval times, have their own particular moral outlook. In this, and in the presence of a considerable amount of symbolism and Buddhist idealism from the continent, they display a trend different from that of Heian literature. Yet they too, in their own Buddhistic way, show a tendency to dwell on the inevitable decline of the mighty which gives them a kind of humanistic bent. Again, the *kyōgen* farces which appeared alongside the Nō carry on to a considerable degree the same trends as the purely Japanese literature of the previous age, and deal with

the daimyos and landlords of the day with a satirical touch reminiscent of Molière.

In its dramatic dialogue, its costumes, and its stage setting, the Nō incorporated continental influences, yet the ways in which it differs from its continental models illustrate well the characteristic forms taken by Japanese culture. The Kabuki of the Tokugawa period also owes much to the Chinese drama, but its gestures and elocution diverge sharply from those of the continent; the esthetic sensibility is far more delicate, and both the libretti and the staging achieved an independent development. (Admittedly, the Kabuki, being an art of the merchant class which stood culturally at a comparatively low level, tended to lack the classic elegance which the aristocrats of the Heian period and the priests of the period of samurai rule achieved in adopting continental originals to the Japanese taste; to replace the more grotesque continental elements with a Japanese-type restraint was not sufficient to make it truly Japanese—though it is this very failure that gives Kabuki its "Oriental" quality so beloved of foreigners.)

Chikamatsu Monzaemon (1653–1724), who has been called the "Shakespeare of Japan," was born at a time when the Kabuki was beginning to acquire a more modern flavor, and by taking as his theme the clash between the morality of the samurai age and the emotions of the modern, bourgeois age, he produced a modern literature corresponding to the renaissance of literature which was occurring in other parts of the world at the time. The literature evolved by the rising bourgeois society of the day complemented the *kogaku*—the revival of the study of the purely Japanese classics— by reviving in comparatively clear-cut form the trends of the literature of the Heian period. The literature had quite a lot in common with European literature of the age of humanism, and Saikaku, who was one of its leading lights, was the precursor of the naturalistic literature of modern Japan.

Here again, however, the conservative tendency of the Japanese

82

made itself felt, and the "modern" novels were at first invariably written in a classical style. Saikaku's own work was in this style, and during the literary renaissance of the Meiji era, which was stimulated by the literature of the West, modern novels again appeared which were written in the language of the classics. In the Edo period, however, its place was eventually taken by a more modern style, or by novels written in the colloquial language of the day, and in the same way the classical style in the Meiji era was soon replaced by the modern colloquial language.

The tea ceremony is often cited in illustration of the spiritual and formal characteristics of Japanese culture, so there is no need to discuss it in detail here. Originating in the tea-drinking ritual of the monasteries of China, in Japan it was first performed in the residences of the daimyo. It subsequently spread to bourgeois society as well, by which time it had assumed a completely opposite aspect, the setting changing to a small, independent teahouse resembling a rustic cottage where samurai and merchant enjoyed the ritual drinking of tea on completely equal terms.

The tea ceremony became extremely formalized, and the highly cultivated tastes brought to bear on it made it in practice a somewhat expensive, even extravagant pastime; yet, paradoxically enough, it clung throughout to its theoretical rejection of formalism and luxury in any form. The paradox, however, was one which had existed in the literary outlook of the upper classes in Japan since ancient times: the aristocratic poems and romances of the Heian period had at one and the same time exalted and criticized the self, while even the merchant class in Tokugawa times had shown in its novels an almost Dickensian tendency simultaneously to glory in and poke fun at itself.

5

A fact that should never be overlooked in considering Japanese cul-

ture is that in most of its aspects it is not something created by a class of intellectuals divorced from the atmosphere of society as a whole, but is a direct product of that atmosphere itself. This truth, so often missed by students of Japanese culture, is in reality of the greatest importance.

The first Japanese literature to appear in ancient times was a product of aristocratic society, yet its roots lay in society as a whole. Its ideas and emotions were also, therefore, those of society as a whole, and aristocratic literature found a ready understanding even at the lowest levels of society. Only a few people in the upper reaches of society read the *Tale of Genji* in the original, yet its contents were known through popular picture-books and woodblock prints as late as the Tokugawa period. The martial literature of the medieval age similar found its propagators in the professional story-tellers, and the tales of the medieval warriors were known throughout every class of society.

The Kabuki, an art of the bourgeoisie aimed at the merchants and artisans, was of course familiar to the point where every shop apprentice and craftsman could do vocal imitations of the finest Kabuki artists. Teachers of instrumental and vocal music in the Tokugawa period drew their pupils principally from merchant and artisan classes. It was this type of person who had the truest appreciation of the best in both drama and music. The ukiyo-e, which in the Western view requires a discerning taste to appreciate, was in fact a product of the popular taste of Tokugawa times. The homes of merchants and craftsmen possessed bound volumes of many of those prints which the European collector today prizes so highly, and they were familiar playthings for their children.

The birth from among the masses of arts of such high quality, and their enjoyment by the masses, was made possible by the fact that education utilizing the *kana* syllabary and the spoken word had given large numbers of Japanese, in an age without public educational institutions, a comparatively consistent degree of civilization. Even

those Japanese who could not read or write were given factual and emotional education via the non-official media of oral culture— which, although they were in fact media for popular entertainment, told in an extremely artistic manner tales with substantially the same content as the histories and romances of literature. The arts of the age were without exception aimed at the masses, and the fact that the arts themselves, such as the ukiyo-e and the Kabuki, were able to attain a considerably high level was due to the oral education which the ordinary Japanese had been receiving since ancient times. In short, Japan in the Edo period had an extraordinary educational system which was at once organized and unorganized, a system in which literature written in the *kana* script was available to all, and in which those who could not read were supplied with it in oral form.

The fact that *tanka* and *haiku* (the 31-syllable and 17-syllable verse forms) were written in larger quantities by ordinary people than by specialist poets—a state of affairs unparalleled in any other country —can also be attributed to the same reasons. However much the poetry of the professional poet is a product of his refined literary sensibility, that work must, in the long run, find its roots in the popular cultural level of the age. Those untranslatable terms *wabi* and *sabi*, used to express the plain, rustic, superficially almost crude taste apparent in the tea ceremony, were taken over by the *haiku* also; they represent the expression of a highly sophisticated cultural awareness in extremely unsophisticated, artless terms. They have been explained theoretically in terms of Buddhist or Taoist philos- ophy, but in fact they are an outcome of a perfectly ordinary frame of mind—common to all Japanese, whether aristocrat or warrior, tradesman or craftsman—which expresses the self in deprecating, or even in negative, terms. The same frame of mind is apparent not only in Japanese literature and art, but in Japanese customs, man- ners, and language as well. It is paralleled by the unique method of voice production in Japanese music, which uses the whole capacity

of the lungs to produce a voice which in itself lies somewhere in the medium range of the voice—a process known as "stealing" or "killing" the voice. The highest forms of Japanese culture are dominated by the same general tendency, a tendency which is one of the most basic criteria in discriminating what is specifically Japanese from what is common to other nations.

V THE PSYCHOLOGICAL CHARACTERISTICS
OF THE JAPANESE

I

The mental and emotional qualities of the Japanese, like those of most highly developed nations, are extremely diverse. A Japanese discussing the psychological makeup of his own race tends accordingly to stress those aspects which he possesses himself and to overlook the other aspects. The observations of a foreigner, which similarly tend to be weighted in favor of those aspects which have impressed themselves most strongly on him personally, often produce precisely the opposite judgement.

The situation is complicated by the fact that the Japanese combine a rather Latin taste for extremes with an almost Anglo-Saxon pragmatism. They are progressive, and at the same time conservative; at one moment they seem to be peace-loving, at another bellicose. Each of these aspects, moreover, is in itself quite strong. Viewed historically, however, the Japanese as a race have run to extremes on comparatively few occasions. Very often an individual, or a group, or a district has shown itself ultra-conservative or ultra-radical, but seldom has the race, the nation as a whole, overstepped the mark.

One of the most conspicuous features of the Japanese seen in the light of social psychology is their capacity to incorporate conflicting psychological trends within the same age, the same region, or the same group. Unless this fact is recognized, there is a danger of misinterpreting both the Japanese psychology and Japanese history. This capacity is probably due to the large number of races with different characteristics that went into the making of the Japanese. Similarly,

the middle-of-the-road course taken by Japanese history, its avoidance of extremes, is without doubt another outcome of this synthesis of varied elements. All partial characteristics are synthesized or cancel each other out, until they form a homogeneous whole.

2

In their individual psychology also, the Japanese sometimes combine different traits within the same person, but the trend is still more marked when they are considered as a racial, social, or class entity. The samurai of the feudal period, considered both as a class and as individuals, showed just this juxtaposition of opposite extremes. Okakura Tenshin, who expounded the Japanese character and ethic for the foreign reader with considerable truth, if rather over-poetically, said in *The Awakening of Japan,* ''The samurai, like his weapon, was cold, but never forgot the fire in which he was forged.'' Indeed, even in the medieval age, an age of violent armed strife, the samurai found in ''coldness'' both his courage and his morality. Okakura says in explanation of this that ''in the feudal days Zen had taught him self-restraint and made courteousness the mark of bravery.'' In fact, however, the ''cold'' aspect of the Japanese *samurai* came less from his training in the continental Zen than from the native psychology. In Japan, Zen was considered necessary for the samurai less as a way of inculcating self-restraint than as a way of maintaining his presence of mind in an emergency; the sang-froid of the samurai was confined neither to the age when Zen was fashionable nor to the warrior class only. One recalls the celebrated myth telling how in the prehistoric age a god of martial valor who lost his self-restraint was driven out by a council of the other gods. The view that self-restraint and courtesy were signs of courage was part of the Japanese ethic even in ancient times, and in later ages it remained a characteristic of the outlook of the well-bred Japanese. As we shall see later,

88

this value placed on self-restraint also found expression in the various manifestations of Japanese culture.

3

At crucial times in Japanese history it has invariably been possible to detect the characteristics of the Japanese psychology just discussed. A not inconsiderable portion of the Japanese are prone to occasional impulsive or fanatical attitudes, yet not once so far have such lapses into extremity caused confusion at any vital point in history. At the really crucial times, the Japanese have always maintained their self-restraint and ability to think again.

Even in the age of samurai government, the samurai themselves retained this restraint of outlook. The Hōjōs, for example, continued to serve the Ashikaga shoguns in the capacity of retainers even after they had established what was, in fact, a political dictatorship. They were held back by traditional, social forces transcending the merely political. It is typical of one aspect of the Japanese mentality that the Hōjōs should thus have been curbed by supra-military forces even in an age when military might was apparently what counted above all. Admittedly, to ignore the force of tradition would, as in other similar cases, have been to imperil the Hōjōs' own interests as well, but supra-political, supra-military considerations could not have functioned in restraining a class which judged everything in terms of military strength without a considerable predisposition in that direction in that class's own mentality. So in the age of the ascendancy of the Taira family, the same clan produced both a Kiyomori and a Shigemori to hold him in check.   58

The same characteristics were very much in evidence at the time of the Meiji Restoration. Even the overthrow of the Tokugawa government which had held centralized control for almost three centuries occasioned no more serious opposition than came from two or

three daimyos, and came nowhere near causing any serious national schism. Alongside the more obvious explanations for this must be accounted the fact that the daimyo and samurai of the day still retained the combination of self restraint and good sense peculiar to the Japanese people.

Where restraint is not accompanied by wisdom it easily becomes cowardice and escapism. In important periods for the Japanese, the restraint was fortunately accompanied by this wisdom in comparatively high degree. For example, at the time when antagonism had arisen between the court and the Tokugawa government, Napoleon III suggested that France should give the Tokugawa government military or financial aid, but Tokugawa government officials who were in France at the time advised the government to reject the offer. The government, of course, showed no hesitation in refusing such risky foreign help—indeed, it was itself about to take the courageous move of returning the reins of government to the Emperor. Here is another example of the combination of self-restraint and wisdom shown by Japanese at crucial times. The same psychology was shown 1,300 years earlier, at the time of the Taika Reform, when the elimination of a single man, the head of the aristocratic Soga family which had held autocratic power over a period of several generations, was enough to accomplish the major task of returning power to the court and establishing a centralized government without causing any civil disturbance.

4

As we have seen already, an unpractical love of extremes is matched in the Japanese personality by a practical dislike of those same extremes. Despite a tendency for the former to be admired as idealistic and the latter to be vilified as excessively down-to-earth, it is the

latter that has directed the main trends of Japanese history. The famous episode at the time of the Meiji Restoration when an attack on Edo Castle was averted by a meeting between Saigō Takamori and Katsu Kaishū, leaders of the imperial and Tokugawa forces respectively, is a good example of the Japanese mentality. Among the imperial forces there were many who advocated a military blow against the Tokugawa, while similar thinkers on the Tokugawa side, who were opposed to the peaceful handing over of Edo Castle by Katsu, actually entrenched themselves at Ueno, where they joined battle with the imperial forces. Moreover, these rebels received general sympathy for their reckless valor and stubbornness in the face of impossible odds—pure bravery, in other words, which resisted to the end, hopelessly, without a thought of self-interest. They were hailed as "true Edo samurai," while Katsu, who was himself a pure Edo samurai, was criticized for lack of the "Edo spirit" and for showing an excessively realistic, calculating approach. Even Fukuzawa Yukichi, one of the most progressive and modern thinkers among the pioneers of the Meiji era, was concerned at the effect Katsu's excessively "realistic" attitude might have on the toughness and fortitude that formed another aspect of the Japanese character. And yet, Katsu was an "Edo samurai" through and through. It was he who had captained the first Western-style Japanese warship ever to cross the Pacific to America without any aid from foreigners. He resolutely followed through what he believed to be the right course of action, handing Edo Castle over to the imperial forces despite several threats of assassination, and remaining unshaken by pressure put on him by Tokugawa samurai and others whose courage was greater than their wisdom. The politicians and military men who fell victim to the frequent assassinations of post-Meiji times were possessed of the same mental courage as Katsu. Katsu was in no way inferior to most samurai in military courage: he was superior to them, in fact, in that in him brute courage was tempered by restraint

allied to wisdom. In short, he was a typical samurai and a typical Japanese, and it is the attitude that he typifies which has generally prevailed at crucial moments in Japanese history.

5

Nevertheless, there is no gainsaying that the Japanese mentality has its rash, thoughtless side as well, which is generally numbered along with impetuosity, instability, and lack of perseverance and staying-power, as one of the failings of the Japanese makeup. Some supporters of the "milieu" theory suggest that these failures of the national character are due to the influence of natural surroundings. The islands of Japan stretch far from north to south, and cover a wide range of climate, from the frigid to the sub-tropical. The central portion, indeed, has a temperate climate, but its topography—a long, narrow strip of territory pierced down its length by steep mountain ranges from which the land slopes sharply away to the Japan Sea on one side and the Pacific Ocean on the other—is such that flat land is scarce. With a few exceptions, the rivers are shallow and swift, so that the heavy rainfall frequently causes them to overflow. On top of these unsettling geographical and topographical features, damage from volcanos and earthquakes is frequent, while typhoons and other storms brewed in the south Pacific often come to wreak havoc in Japan. Such natural conditions, it is argued, are hardly conducive of a relaxed, unhurried disposition; thus the Japanese tend to be preoccupied with the momentary rather than the eternal; they are clever, but lack spiritual weight and dignity; and they have various other psychological failings of a kindred nature. To the same causes are attributed the excessive susceptibility of the Japanese to external stimuli, their consequent proneness to blind imitation, and other such aspects not to be found in a really great nation.

92

Yet as we have already seen, the tendency of the Japanese mentality to fly to extremes, or to lack staying-power, is by no means predominant; Japanese history has never been sacrificed to it at the most crucial periods. It is more common, at such periods, for the conciliatory outlook, born of patience and self-control, to win the day over the more impetuous, exclusionist outlook.

To stretch a simile rather, one might compare this conciliatory outlook to the way natural conditions in Japan combine a complex of many and diverse elements into an integrated natural beauty. Some have seen in this outlook a type of resignation—an ability to submit placidly to the worst fate can bring—fostered in the Japanese by the pressure of harsh natural conditions. This is a mistaken view. The outlook in question does not indicate a readiness to give up but, as in the case of Katsu, the suppression of incidentals out of consideration for the whole, which happens to produce an effect similar to resignation.

What the West refers to as "Oriental resignation" is a psychological tendency to be seen in such peoples of the Euroasian mainland as the Indians, the Chinese, and the Russians. It is the mentality of peoples who find themselves constantly up against something vast and overbearing in nature or in social forms; it is not the mentality of the Japanese. Nature in Japan runs wild at times, but in its normal state it is moderate, and lacks the oppressive quality of nature on the continent. The machinery of state, too, lacks the massiveness and coerciveness of the empire-states of the continent, and tends, even, to the cozily domestic—a tendency aptly symbolized by the architecture of the Imperial Palace in Kyoto. Social forms, too, match Japanese domestic architecture in their love of the small-scale, and in taking a refined simplicity as their ideal. With a state and a society of this type, the Japanese have never found themselves forced into an attitude of resignation. One might go farther and say, even, that for the same reason they tend not to know when to give up. Along

with their ready acceptance of realities, they also show a distinct reluctance to give up an idea that has taken them.

In the feudal age, for example, the ease with which the Tokugawas succeeded in unifying the country was due to the unexpected willingness to help them shown after Toyotomi's death by large numbers of daimyos who, if only they had chosen either separately or in concert to oppose the Tokugawas, could have put up at least a resistance of sorts. Whatever their motives, there were very few daimyos who were sufficiently rash or sufficiently enamored of lost causes to oppose the Tokugawas to the death—a fact which irritated some later and more idealistic historians. Yet, given the benefit of the doubt, their action, too, may well be seen as prompted by a mixture of self-restraint and wisdom. Though their thinking might, perhaps, be accused of self-interest, it was certainly not "resignation." It is interesting, incidentally, that many of the fiefs which at that time felt compelled to make concessions on behalf of the Tokugawas were anti-Tokugawa at the time of the Meiji Restoration. As historians have pointed out, this betrays a desire for revenge for what they had put up with three centuries earlier and in the intervening years; in short, it is a good example of the working in the Japanese mentality of the precise opposite of "resignation."

6

The psychological characteristics of the Japanese as revealed in their history naturally find many counterparts in the nation's cultural forms. In the products of their culture, the Japanese, despite a tendency to run to extremes, usually end up with a kind of happy mean. In the same way, their progressive aspects are matched by a strong conservatism. In architecture, for example, as we have already seen, the ancient age imitated Chinese styles, producing works such as the Hōryū-ji which in artistic effect even surpass the originals, yet the

same age also created the *shinden-zukuri*, that uniquely Japanese style of architecture. In the eleventh and twelfth centuries, after long years in which the only written literature available to the Japanese was in Chinese, they produced a purely Japanese literature differing from the latter in form, content, and general tradition alike. Again, the warrior society of the Middle Ages borrowed from the philosophy, literature, art, and every other aspect of the culture of the China of Sung times and later, but almost all of them were made over into forms based on a Japanese, rather than a Chinese, sensibility and psychology. Despite all talk of a lack of cultural forms purely Japanese in origin, these Japanized forms, in their underlying feeling, were in fact unique.

The underlying "Japanese" traits are often summed up in the West by adjectives such as "simple," "plain," "moderate," "natural," or "realistic." All are correct. These qualities, which have much in common with the self-restraint apparent throughout Japanese history, show themselves in the products of Japanese culture as an underlying tendency to restrain and refine the stronger emotions and more primitive reactions. The preference for a subdued, implicit beauty over an explicit, showy beauty, or for an inner beauty to an outward beauty, can be seen as part of the same trend. Another example of this characteristic Japanese mentality is seen in women's clothes, where aggressive colors such as are worn by women in the West or Southeast Asia are avoided in external garments, which are mostly in neutral colors, bright colors being reserved for the undergarments.

The esthetic sense of the Japanese, despite certain resemblances to Greek classicism, rejects the idealized, symmetrical and perfect beauty of the Greeks in favor of a more natural, assymmetrical, and incomplete beauty. The well-known *Book of Tea* by Okakura Tenshin attributes this Japanese love of the assymmetrical and incomplete to the influence of medieval Zen. Here again, however, he is led astray by his own personal inclinations. The tendency to see

95

beauty in the assymmetrical, far from being a product of the samurai age, is apparent in a building as ancient as the Izumo Shrine, built long before Zen ever came to Japan. The love of the incomplete can also be detected, in both the moral and formal senses, in literature of the ancient period such as the *Kojiki* and *Manyōshū*. Motoori Norinaga, the pioneer of the study of the Japanese classics, pointed out that ancient literature such as the *Kojiki, Manyōshū,* and *Tale of Genji* was not dominated by any artificial "perfect morality." It is true that love of the imperfect as the type of Japanese formal beauty finds its most vital expression in the rituals and architecture of the tea ceremony, developed in the middle ages and later, but even here the dominating influence was not so much that of Zen and the ways of life of the Zen priesthood, as the taste for the rustic life which developed, along with the growth of bourgeois society in Japan, as a reaction against the aristocratic and samurai ways of life. Its psychological roots lay in a preference for a natural, imperfect type of beauty over the artificially perfect, and despite all their stylization the architecture of the tea room, its garden, the utensils used in the ceremony, and even its formalized movements and language, all show, in their essential spirit, the same reverence for nature.

VI THE JAPANESE NATION AND
TRADITIONAL ATTITUDES

I

A nation, one might say, does not really have traditions; rather, it is the traditional motivations and behavior that, in themselves, constitute what is normally meant by a "nation." The concept of "nation," again, is usually associated with that of "race," but most nations, considered ethnologically, are extremely diverse, and there is almost no civilized state consisting of a group of individuals of a single ethnic origin. It is, rather, an identical set of inherited ways of life, in the broad sense, that gives us our idea of nation. Provided the heritage is identical, differences of racial origin are soon forgotten, and even elements which, historically speaking, are clearly known to be foreign come to suffer no discrimination whatsoever. An example in Japan is the way that descendants of the immigrants known as *hambetsu* have become Japanese like everybody else. On the other hand, where the inherited ways of life are different, then racial discrimination persists even where the two groups are mixed together in the same area and share the same relations. Within the Chinese people, which is made up of many nations and races, there are some areas where assimilation of traditions has done away with awareness of distinctions, while in others—as in the case of the Chinese Muslims—their persistence has led to the retention of separate national forms and ideas.

One may inquire here whether the nation persists because its heritage is preserved, or whether the heritage is preserved because of the continuance of the nation. The Jews in Europe are considered,

even today, to constitute a special racial entity of their own, and this is usually attributed to the way they cling to their own special ways of life. However, the preservation of those ways of life can also be attributed to the fact that, forming groups within other nations with no home country of their own, they have always been viewed by those countries as aliens, with the result that they have had to strengthen their unity by preserving their traditional ways of life and continuing the occupational, social, or guild-type communal forms handed down from their fathers—deliberately continuing, in other words, some forms to distinguish them from others. There are not a few cases in history where special inherited ways of life have been preserved, not out of any special need of the people as such, but because of class or occupational discriminations against them. [Note: the state of Israel has been formed since this was written.]

The nation as a unit with a particular way of life has a special set of inherited forms which distinguish it from other units and which give rise to the idea of the nation as an absolute in much the same way as the modern concept of the individual; they create, in other words, the idea of a unique and irreplaceable national "self." Inherited ways of life are a tangible expression of this national self and serve to maintain the uniqueness of the nation's life as a whole. Why, one may ask, should a nation be obliged to preserve a way of life different from that of others? The answer, of course, is that intercourse among the varied ways of life of different nations is one of the conditions for the betterment of human life as a whole, in just the same way that the uniqueness of the individual is a necessary condition for the improvement of the human race. Civilization, like the species, is born of an intermingling of different ways of life, and variety among the nations which act as the "units" of civilization is one of its basic prerequisites.

Tradition is the handing-down from generation to generation of ways of life in the sense just described. It represents, thus, a special, enduring quality affecting all aspects of civilization from the various

tangible cultural forms to the intangible activities of the mind and spirit. The heritage, moreover, takes the form of an intuitive and supra-intellectual compulsion.

Tradition is characterized by the sense of superiority by which it is accompanied in its owner. There is no nation which is not convinced of the superiority of its own tradition; the "nation," in fact, is the joint protector both of its tradition and of the sense of superiority that goes with it. Objectively speaking, of course, there are no standards existing outside the traditions of one nation or another by which one can determine which is the superior. It very commonly occurs, moreover, that two traditions have diametrically opposed sets of values, what is a virtue in one being considered a vice in the other; this gives a great variety to national characters, a variety which contributes to the development of the whole. Although this interplay of "vices" and "virtues" forms an incentive to progress, the sense of superiority always implicit in the culture of a particular nation is also a necessary psychological condition for the preservation of its special forms—it parallels, as it were, the idea of the "absoluteness" of the individual.

The preservation of a culture, therefore, is an unconscious phenomenon, a kind of supra-conscious compulsion. Even where a particular culture is handed on consciously, with full awareness of its values, there is always at the bottom an unconscious, compulsive element. The sense of superiority accompanying a tradition is itself a working of this unconscious mental process. It goes with the necessity of the preservation of the culture which, however it may seem to be the result of intellectual judgement, is not really so in fact. The traditional English ethic, for example, emphasizes a particular type of stolidity. The English are proud of it to the extent that they attribute to it the particular English brand of conservatism, and it is, accordingly, passed on consciously from father to son. Where actual ways of life are concerned, however, the conservatism is supra-conscious in the extreme; and it is precisely this that makes it

so essential a part of the English spirit. The continuity of their political systems, the sturdiness and resilience of their social mores are not the outcome, but the cause of, their more theoretical conservatism. The way the English, say, take a fancy to the oil lamp just when the gas lamp puts in its appearance, or cling to the gas lamp when electric light is invented, is one manifestation of a stubbornness of spirit which affects not just the aristocracy but the nation as a whole. Although the tradition undoubtedly has its value as part of the national character, English pride in it stems less from an intellectual assessment of its worth than from an irrational, almost physiological need.

It is irrational feelings such as these that play the chief part in the continuance of tradition. Nor is this particular mental trait restricted to the English, but affects every nation to a greater or lesser extent. The same kind of thing is also detectable, of course, in the literary and other fields. Even the conscious carrying-on of ancient forms seen in the neo-classical styles of Meiji literature was basically motivated by an unconscious sense of the superiority of the tradition. This kind of conservatism, affecting all aspects of civilization and deriving from the unconscious conviction of the superiority of the native culture, reveals itself in what is known as ''traditionalism.''

2

''Traditionalism'' considered as the preservation of the national identity is present in every nation and in every individual, to the extent that it can almost be called a kind of instinct. It may not be an instinct of the kind that makes the chick start pecking at the soil as soon as it emerges from the shell, but it is a general trend in behavior in the broad sense of the word, a trend similar to that which makes people speaking a particular language do so with the same word-sounds and rhythms.

No progress whatsoever is possible through rigid adherence to a simple traditional outlook, but equally impossible is progress without any basis of tradition. The development of language, for example, takes place strictly in accordance with the traditions of a particular tongue. Individuals may learn to speak a foreign tongue well, but this is quite separate from the development of their native tongue by assimilation of outside influences. Similarly, the technique of producing the sounds of a foreign language mechanically, without relation to the traditional qualities of one's own language, is quite different from the refinement, by a process of development and assimilation, of the sounds and rhythms of the latter itself. Here too, things foreign merely serve as materials for development based on the indigenous, traditional sounds and rhythms.

The same kind of thing can be said of everything connected with art. Western-style painting is of the same general type throughout all the countries of the white races, while Oriental painting all tends to follow a basically Chinese pattern. Despite this apparently international character of most culturally developed forms of artistic expression, even countries as closely related as those of Europe each have their own unique manner. What invests the painting of each country with its own national individuality is the general *manner* in which the cultural forms of that country are transmitted from generation to generation. In other words, the possession of a tradition permeating the culture as a whole gives distinctive national flavors to arts stemming from one and the same stock.

3

The importance of tradition in culture does not mean that the ways of life of the past should be carried on quite unaltered, nor would to do so be to preserve tradition in the proper sense. Even supposing, for example, it proved possible to maintain the Nō drama for

century after century in precisely the form in which it was known in Ashikaga times, this would not be a proper expression of tradition. It would be comparable to the excavation of objects buried in the earth in ancient times, rather than the inheriting of a form as a true "tradition." Tradition's role lies not so much in the preservation of the cultural properties of the past in their original form as in giving shape to contemporary culture; not in the retention of things as they were, but in the way certain national qualities inherent in them live on in the contemporary culture.

Thus if a contemporary writer were to produce works exactly similar to the prose romances of the Heian period, it would undoubtedly constitute a "handing-on" in one sense, but it would not mean that the cultural forms of the past were living, as a tradition, in the present. It would be a mere technical imitation, analogous to the production of ancient objects in a museum.

When traditionalism degenerates into a clinging to the prototypes of past civilization, whether in society, art, or letters, it loses all its point. To do just this, it must be admitted, is the most basic and instinctive inclination of the traditional mentality, yet if traditionalism is to be of the right type it must seek, rather, to free itself from the originals of the past and find itself anew in the present, at the same time taking over sufficient of the heritage of the past to ensure the retention of the national individuality. In the arts, a pupil is not considered to have inherited the spirit of his master until he has ceased to imitate him and recreated what he has learnt within himself. In the same way, the heritage of the past cannot be called a tradition until it has dismissed its prototypes and been reborn in new forms.

It is the same in politics as in the arts. "Traditionalism" in politics tends to turn out as stubborn conservatism, but a true political tradition is carried on via political evolution. The smooth process of development which Japan underwent following the Meiji Restoration, despite the considerable haste with which Western-influenced

reforms were undertaken, owed much to the existence within the Japanese political tradition of a political "spirit" which was resuscitated in the new Meiji political system. It was only when this spirit was allowed to come to life that tradition in the true sense came into operation. At the time of the Restoration, there was stubborn resistance from the "traditionalists," yet paradoxically, the sweeping aside of this opposition and the development of a new system represented, not the defeat of tradition, but the application of its innermost elements to the shaping of a new regime. It also meant, of course, that the new system developed in Japan assumed a form distinct from anything found in the modern history of the West. Such a distinctiveness is natural in any country with pretensions to a basic heritage of its own, and is what gives a nation's history its unique quality.

Great Britain and France afford a good example of the way political traditions can give identical political forms distinctive national characteristics. Although France based its own parliamentary government on forms originally developed in England, the national assembly soon split up into minority parties, and a two-party system of the English type failed to materialize. The question of course is in reality much more complicated than this suggests, but the basic difference in development undoubtedly sprang from a difference between the political traditions of the two countries. And these in turn, one might infer, derived from inherited social forms, i.e., from a whole complex of inherited ways of life. For the same reason, one could see the trend toward a two-party system in the Japanese Diet as deriving from a basic dualistic trend in the Japanese political tradition. Indeed, the same dualistic trend is apparent not only in the nation's political history but in its social history as well. For this reason, it would be no mistake to associate the two-party system in Japan with the rivalry between the two great capitalist blocs in the post-Meiji industrial world, and in the same way the tendency toward a dichotomy which occurs constantly throughout Japanese

history at critical periods—Soga-Mononobe, Minamoto-Taira, Toyotomi-Tokugawa, Kyoto-Edo—should be seen as a political manifestation of something which has its counterpart in the social sphere as well. If one agrees such an inherited tendency exists, then it, too, should be counted as a tradition.

4

If one considers the relationship between a people and its tradition in this light, it is clear that although the characteristic traits of a national tradition reveal themselves in the nature of what is transmitted, what really defines them is the manner of that transmission. Those traits, in short, are qualities inherent in cultural "forms" in the less specific sense, and the characteristic features of national be-behavior—i.e., particular patterns of national behavior—are likewise related ultimately to the traditional features characterizing the nation's political and cultural forms.

It follows that a study of the manner in which the Japanese have handed on their cultural forms will throw light on the peculiarities of the national character as such. In what follows I have tried, in my own way, to throw some light on the national outlook by this means.

The starting-point for Japanese culture was imitation of the culture of the continent. However, imitation in this sense takes place in every country; whether the result is a true culture of the country in question or merely skillful imitation depends on the way the taking-over is carried out. In reality, of course, the distinction is a very difficult one to make. It is far from easy, for example, to say whether the architecture of the Hōryū-ji is a piece of skillful imitation or a genuinely Japanese cultural expression. The specialist, of course, would doubtless point out all kinds of Japanese features in it. At the same time, it is also beyond doubt that in its overall form it follows continental models: however much the Japanese sensi-

bility is at work, so long as that sensibility finds expression in mere details, then the buildings should be classified as technical imitation rather than original creativity. It should be pointed out here, however, that the ability to make an imitation at such a very high level can, in itself, only be attributed to Japan's own cultural heritage. Just as the development of Western-style political forms in post-Meiji Japan depended on an inherited political tradition of thousands of years, so the success of the Nara period in taking over foreign forms of a very highly developed type was only possible because of Japan's own, already existing cultural heritage, which can be seen at work beneath the imitations of foreign culture and which, in itself, represents one kind of tradition.

It is clear, thus, that tradition is at work even in the imitation of foreign cultures. However, the operation of tradition is at such a basic level in a case such as that of the Hōryū-ji that it is overlaid by the more tangible aspects of the cultural forms. There are other cases, on the contrary, in which tradition, though nourished by the influence of foreign cultures, finds its embodiment in novel outward forms. To take an example from architecture again, one recalls the *shinden-zukuri* style of residential architecture which emerged in the same age as the Hōryū-ji. This style is almost the antithesis of that of the Hōryū-ji, and most people would not hesitate to say that it, rather than the Hōryū-ji, represents a continuation of the genuine Japanese cultural heritage.

It has happened, thus, that in one and the same period Japan has succeeded in producing both superior technical imitations and characteristic cultural forms of its own. These are, in fact, simply manifestations of the negative and positive sides, respectively, of the same tradition. In the continental-style architecture it functions covertly as the technical ability to imitate, while in the *shinden-zukuri* it functions overtly to produce a unique cultural form. It is somewhat misleading, perhaps, to refer to these aspects as "negative" and "positive," but it should at least be evident that continuation

of a tradition by no means implies the preservation of the civilization of the previous age just at it stands.

Furthermore, it also becomes clear that the really essential things in a national tradition are carried on by the nation at a level transcending the individual consciousness. Most Japanese, if asked, would point to the Hōryū-ji rather than *shinden-zukuri* architecture as representing the more highly developed cultural form. Admittedly, since the Hōryū-ji is a temple, a "public" edifice quite different in spirit from ordinary dwellings, the criteria by which they pass judgement are doubtless different. Yet even so, it is beyond doubt that the Hōryū-ji has always been more highly admired. All the more, then, would one have expected it to have had a powerful influence in some way or other on the basic approach of the Japanese to their own architecture at the time. At the very least, one would have expected the aristocracy of the day, reared in the continental outlook as they were, to have displayed more of a continental sensibility in the cultural forms of their everyday lives, and to have been influenced somewhat more by the continent in the architecture of their own homes. In practice, the buildings they produced were in complete contrast. The *shinden-zukuri*, of course, doubtless shows a certain continental influence in its layout and elsewhere, but its architectural motifs and its basic treatment stand in contrast to the continental style in every way.

This affords a good clue as to the way the Japanese carry on their tradition. It reveals, as it were, a kind of traditional stubbornness: for all their power to digest foreign cultures, the Japanese have insisted on preserving their own independent forms. In every country, of course, the national conservatism of the race which exists among the mass of the people leads them to cling to regional cultural forms, but it is significant in a somewhat different way that an aristocratic society, brought up on a foreign civilization, should have clung to the particular heritage of its own land in the cultural forms in which it found true self-expression.

This conservatism of the Japanese is particularly stubborn where things closely affecting their daily lives are concerned. Once the purely Japanese style of architecture developed in the Nara period had been brought to perfection in the Heian period, it was perpetuated with almost no new developments of note. This is especially true of Shintō architecture, but even the domestic architecture of today derives from the same basic spirit. That the aristocracy of an age under the virtually absolute dominance of Chinese style should have created an indigenous architectural style is itself a sign of conservatism, while the fact that the style thus created should have been perpetuated for the next thousand years suggests that the creativity was, culturally speaking, of a high order.

5

The same kind of thing is apparent in literature also. A purely Japanese literature did not come into being until the Japanese had already attained quite a high level in Chinese-style literature. Even before this, however, they had achieved considerable success in the imitation of continental culture; there were women, even, who could write perfectly acceptable Chinese verse, and it would seem that education in Chinese studies was widespread among the aristocracy.

Nevertheless, just as the *shinden-zukuri* style of residential architecture was something quite distinct from the style represented by the Hōryū-ji, so the first purely Japanese literature was completely distinct in style from the literature written in Chinese. Official documents and historical records in the age before there was any way of writing Japanese were written in Chinese, probably by immigrant Chinese or their descendants, but in time the Japanese acquired the ability to use Chinese characters themselves. They wrote in pure Chinese with the exception of Japanese ballads quoted in the text, for which Chinese characters were used, irrespective of their

sense, to represent the Japanese sounds. This inevitably meant that the better-quality literature of the educated class consisted exclusively of Chinese prose and poetry.

Even so, when first it was planned to compile an official history of Japan, the method chosen was to have someone familiar with the native oral traditions recite them so that an expert in Chinese literature could transcribe them phonetically in Chinese characters. The result was the *Kojiki*. This seems to have been intended as a preparatory stage in the compilation of a national history in pure Chinese which would put Japan, in her exchanges with the continent, on an equal footing with China. In other words, the real aim was a work of the type of the *Nihon Shoki;* the *Kojiki* was to constitute a kind of collection of source material. Nevertheless, the fact that it was felt necessary, in compiling an official history, first to record the purely Japanese oral traditions can be considered as representing the same type of hankering after tradition as we have already seen in the case of architecture. A similar thing happened at the time of the Meiji Restoration, when the Meiji government approached its task of creating a radically new Western-style system by making a reappraisal of the native tradition, setting up a special bureau which by 1877 had compiled an important history and made a survey of traditional systems of government.

This traditional outlook and spirit played an important part in the emergence of a purely Japanese literature. The creation by the aristocratic society of the Heian period (which already had a high general proficiency in both Chinese prose and Chinese verse) of a phonetic Japanese syllabary based on the Chinese ideographs was a sign that the literary tradition deriving from the primitive oral literature had not been erased by the long years during which Chinese literature had dominated their literary consciousness. Despite all the advances made in the high-grade imitation of foreign literature, it was the primitive literary awareness of the oral tradition that created the *kana* and gave birth to a purely Japanese literature.

6

Having originally no script of its own, Japan retained the old oral literature as its own literary form even after it had attained a fair degree of civilization. The only record we have of it is the *Kojiki*, but it seems safe to infer that there was in fact a considerable body of such literature. Furthermore, it seems likely that it was of greater educational benefit to the Japanese at the time than a written literature would have been, since it could spread among all the people without becoming the monopoly of a small lettered class.

This oral literature seems to have declined greatly following the adoption of Chinese characters; thus the *Kogo Shūi* says, "Since the appearance of writing, people have become loath to talk of ancient matters, manners have become frivolous, and the things of old are actually made fun of." Almost certainly, however, this applied only to the newly literate class, and the education of the common people via tales related by the village elders continued as before. This would seem to have been a major factor in keeping culture in the ancient period comparatively evenly distributed throughout the upper and lower levels of society. Until around the Nara period, Chinese learning, spread though it did, was still restricted to one special section of society. Even the *fubito*—the professional scribes, who were immigrants or descendants of immigrants—were not especially proficient in Chinese literature, so that the average Japanese still had to rely for his education chiefly on the oral literature. This tradition which, as we have seen, was referred to in the compilation of the first national history, was to drive out the techniques of imitating Chinese literature and provide the basis for the growth of a purely Japanese literature some three centuries later. The prose romances that are the earliest form of true Japanese literature inherit the style of the oral recitations of Japan's own ancient age and reject the quasi-Chinese style entirely. This is as true of the type of literary sensibility which they embody as of the formal treatment. In short, in the

Heian period the oral literature of Japan achieved its perfect embodiment in written literature.

Such things as these serve to give an idea of the general outlook
of the Japanese tradition and of the nature of Japanese conservatism.
Although they undeniably reveal a stubborn clinging to the traditional, the high level reached by Japan in the imitation of foreign
culture suggests that the capacities fostered by the native tradition
were not of an exclusionist nature, but of a kind which could be a
fundamental asset in the task of assimilating heterogeneous cultural
forms. To put it in a different way, the Japanese tradition demonstrates a considerable ability to preserve the cultural forms of the
past in their original aspect, yet also to use the heritage of the past as
a basis for the creation of something new.

The explanation for this is doubtless that, although the Japanese
in practice created their own culture via inspirations from foreign
cultures, they themselves constituted from early times a powerful
entity in their own right, both as a nation and as a people. Thus
imitation went hand in hand with self-awareness, and intellectual
recognition of the superiority of foreign civilization with an emotional conviction of the superiority of their own. One sign of this
is the fact that in times when foreign influences were, comparatively
speaking, on the wane, the Japanese promptly set about developing
the cultural forms of foreign origin along indigenous lines rather than
transmitting them as they stood. The transmission of things of foreign origin was transformed into a purely Japanese tradition; thus
the continental manner of reading the Buddhist scriptures gave rise
to the characteristic chanting of the Nō; the purely continental
gagaku was transformed into the music of the Nō, and these in turn
gave rise to the Kabuki.

In the field of literature, we have already seen how the purely
Japanese literature of ancient times achieved independence of Chinese literature. The literature of the middle ages reverted temporarily to a debased imitation of Chinese literature (the decline in

exchanges between the Japanese court and the continent led to a corresponding increase in non-official exchanges, with the result that a class of professional interpreters emerged; it seems possible that this literature derived from the odd brand of Chinese written by these men). It was a refinement of this style, with added influences from the romanticism of Chinese literature, that was responsible for the martial chronicles of medieval Japan. Even during this period, however, the traditional *monogatari* type of literature persisted in the popular tales and novelettes known as *sōshi*, which in turn were to lead to the literary revival of the Edo period seen in the work of Saikaku and others like him. Then, with the naturalist literature of the very end of the Edo period, the same tradition gave rise to a modern literature which, though in a completely different language and written for a completely different class, belonged essentially to the same line as the *monogatari* literature of ancient times.

Right up to the Meiji era, thus, the traditional outlook showed a remarkable consistency. This is clear when one considers, for example, how the literary and artistic revival that occurred under new foreign influences around the middle of that era assumed forms which were in fact a resuscitation of traditional forms—though since then it is apparent that the traditional outlook has begun to undergo something of a transformation (see Chapter III).

existence between the [ ]government and the admission that by a corresponding [ ] more marks [ ] syllables, with a [ ] would [ ] should [ ] persons imprisoned [ ] again [ ] so that the [ ] that the [ ] [ ] been forced [ ] not [ ] of a [ ] pastime [ ]

VII MODES OF EXPRESSION IN JAPANESE CIVILIZATION

In the same way that an individual's words and gestures—not their content, but the forms—give a clue to his character, so general trends in the cultural forms of a nation tell something about the essential nature of that nation's civilization. Once the cultural forms of a nation are seen as concrete expressions of its civilization, then the general atmosphere pervading all forms of cultural expression both spiritual and material—from learning, the arts, and the crafts to language, manners and particular customs—throws direct light on the essence of the civilization of that particular country.

It is often said that Japanese civilization rejects the imposing, the majestic, the complex and the minutely detailed—all characteristics of the continental civilization—in favor of the small-scale perfection, of a refinement which is the ultimate in simplicity and austerity, and of an uncloying, neat type of beauty, and that Japanese civilization therefore lacks the continental grandeur of spirit—that its concrete manifestations are all rather like the wooden houses in which the Japanese live: impermanent, fragile, unexciting, and lacking in power.

Nevertheless, that Japan, though an Oriental nation, should yet demonstrate a Japanese quality so different from that, say, of China, of India, of Persia, or of Turkey, was an inevitable outcome of the national modes of life, irrespective of how that quality might be assessed in the light of other nations' standards. These ways of life, moreover, were such that Japan underwent no national disaster or

social collapse of the kind seen in these other nations, but pursued a steady course of development—which may well suggest that Japanese civilization's basic rejection of the exaggerated and over-elaborate aspects of the civilization of the rest of the world represents, in fact, a desirable working of human restraint.

However much a country's power or wealth increases, it does not necessarily follow that it must adopt the grandiloquent, over-elaborate forms common to the continental civilizations. In one sense, indeed, a cultural refinement which emphasizes the austere, the plain, and the simple is far more "civilized," humanly speaking, than its reverse as seen in continental cultures, though it is obvious, of course, that Japanese civilization also lacks some of the good features of the continental civilizations of East and West. Although the approach of the Japanese has always been to take over the better features of others, and not to insist blindly on the forms of their own civilization, an exception to this approach should be made, I feel, with the grandiloquent and over-elaborate aspects of continental civilization just mentioned. Rather than be dazzled into imitating them, the Japanese should adopt a more critical attitude. The modern Japanese, I feel, have much to learn from their ancestors' refusal—or inability—to take over these particular qualities in anything more than a half-hearted fashion.

The reason why Japanese civilization differs in its basic nature from the continental civilizations of both East and West lies in the natural scene, and in the special nature of the political and social forms which have been handed down over the centuries. Thanks to these, whatever mighty foreign civilization the Japanese came into contact with—however they strove to submit themselves to it—Japan civilization—and specific forms of cultural expression similarly—remained set on its own particular course.

This fact is brought home to me very forcibly every time I see a Japanese castle. Though designed by samurai during the age of

samurai rule, Japanese castles nevertheless illustrate admirably the unique nature of the Japanese sensibility.

Both in the East and the West, the military states of the Middle Ages employed the utmost that the continental culture could offer in size and elaboration of detail in order to vaunt their own power and wealth. So with the feudal state in Japan (even admitted that the accumulation of power and wealth was smaller than in the continental states), one would expect to find something basic in common with the other military states—an exaggeration and proliferation, that is, commensurate with the particular scale of things in Japan. Yet even this was absent from Japan's warrior culture.

In China, the "castle" took the form of ramparts surrounding the whole town. Although there was no central structure, there were enormous and impressive gateways and lookout towers. Japan imitated China in her great temple buildings, for example, yet her castles show no tendency to follow the Chinese model, but are expressions of a purely Japanese sensibility. This is not necessarily because the requirements of war in Japan made the foreign style impracticable. The frequency of earthquakes, of course, doubtless tended to make people avoid the use of stone in building—but even in China, quite a few citadel gates were made of wood. The rejection of the style of Chinese gates and ramparts, in short, would seem to have been dictated not solely by such practical considerations, but also by the essential cultural sensibility of the warrior age.

Although the structure of Japanese castles as such is quite massive —on a "military" scale if allowances are made for the difference of scale as a whole in Japan—the basic treatment reveals the same love of straight lines, simplicity, and austerity as is found in the uniquely Japanese architecture of Shintō shrines. Similarly, the over-all emphasis on white is a return to a characteristically Japanese feeling for color; even Shintō shrines had come to imitate continental styles to the extent of coloring their exteriors vermilion, and

it is a sign of something fundamental in samurai culture that it should have rejected this and relied chiefly on white. The Japanese castle, developed in its most characteristic form only toward the end of the Sengoku age, was certainly not the outcome of any inadequate experience of war, yet in practice it transcended martial considerations and became a kind of model expression of samurai culture. The effect it achieves is less intimidating, in fact, than esthetic.

In the West, there were individual strongholds in addition to walled cities of the Chinese type. These, too, display the same love of grandiloquence and over-elaboration, and in this sense probably represent a more advanced stage in the history of architecture than the Japanese castle. The Japanese castle, however, avoids the artistic temptation to proliferate detail, nor does it follow the Chinese form. Instead, it preserves a typically Japanese simplicity, with the love of the straightforward and classical that was one aspect of the samurai temperament. No one who sees Nagoya Castle soaring above the pine trees growing on the stone ramparts of its outer moat is likely to feel the sense of oppression created by the citadels of China or the castles of Europe. He is more likely, in fact, to find something appealing in its unpretentiousness, in the way it relies entirely for its effect on its simple, symmetrical, straight-lined composition. Indeed, the overall effect created by a Japanese castle with its surrounding moats and grounds is a particularly fine example of what, in the West, would be called landscape gardening. Edo Castle in particular (the present Imperial Palace), a spacious stretch of castle grounds with no soaring keep, presented a magnificent man-made landscape quite without parallel, as the central feature of a city, elsewhere in the world. Even now that it has lost its military significance, it is not merely not in the way, but forms a focal point of the kind that could never be hoped for in a newly-created city.

Even so, what is still more significant than the esthetic value of Japanese castles as such is the fact that it was the samurai culture which gave birth to them. Judged by world standards, the Japanese

castle may represent a comparatively simple and unsophisticated type of cultural expression, yet the fact that in Japan even the culture of the ruling samurai should have maintained such a completely unique quality gives a clue to the basic nature of Japanese civilization as a whole.

The emphasis placed on military might during the age of samurai rule, and the struggle to seize power among the feudal states, plunged Japan into a state of internal strife almost as bad as the interracial struggles in the Chinese state—though again, of course, on a smaller scale, and with the maintenance of a certain degree of order, so that things never reached the parlous state they did in China. Nevertheless, the cultural manifestations of this age were the complete antithesis of the age itself. This was as true of its literature and its art as it was of its helmets and armor, which were affairs of delicate curves and color combinations utterly unlike the intimidating armor of the Chinese or the iron-plated, eminently practical armor of the West.

The same kind of thing is true of the *Heike Monogatari* and *Gempei Seisuiki*, martial chronicles which—though admittedly made use of to some extent for Buddhist propaganda—are different from the heroic tales of old Europe and China in that they represent no cult of the hero but tend to view their principal characters from a tragic viewpoint. So with the period's histories: when the warriors decided to imitate the Nara and Heian periods and produce official histories of the age, the result was not histories in the romantic vein common to other countries in the military age, but works of the type of *Azuma Kagami*, i.e., objective accounts with few other pretensions. The poetry in Japanese of the age similarly showed a delicacy and technical elaboration in striking contrast to the intellectual outlook of warrior society.

One reason for this was that, unlike in China or the countries of the West, the central focus of the national tradition—i.e., the traditional center of the national government—never disappeared, so that

the culture of warrior society had of necessity to imitate the traditional culture of the capital, Kyoto, while the culture of the Kamakura and Muromachi periods was also an imitation of it with modifications. Thanks to this, even during the civil wars, the basic nature of Japanese civilization was not lost sight of.

In fact, this basic nature was emphasized even more strongly, albeit in different forms from before. As we have already seen, although the system of court ranks and the religious culture of the Heian period followed continental models, cultural expression in private life and ordinary society preserved a purely Japanese conciseness and simplicity. Even the dwellings of the aristocracy were plain out of all comparison with the majesty and brilliance of the Buddhist temples, the only thing of which they might boast being a certain refinement of sensibility. In the same way, the culture that was born of the power and wealth of samurai society, far from attempting to imitate continental culture, basically followed the traditional Kyoto forms, merely adapting them to suit the requirements of the samurai age.

There is something almost ironic about these forms. The most "extravagant" forms of culture both in private life and society during the period of samurai rule were neat, well-mannered forms which were small in scale and careful to preserve their refinement of sensibility. The "luxurious" structures of the Muromachi period were in fact cramped buildings such as the Kinkaku-ji (Golden Pavilion) and Ginkaku-ji (Silver Pavilion) in Kyoto. As this trend developed, it became increasingly negative and gave rise to the type of outlook typified by the tea ceremony, which would lavish great sums of money on some imported but unostentatious utensil or other so as to maintain the appearance of rusticity and unpretentiousness.

In this respect, the traditional type of cultural expression in Japan is the opposite of the trend on the mainlands of both East and West, in that the greater the power and wealth becomes the greater is the emphasis on ideals of plainness and modesty. Where increased wealth

and power find expression in forms that are grandiloquent and over-complex in the continental manner, they are rejected as un-Japanese, or at best scorned as representing the taste of the rustic or the par-venu. It is an ironic fact that the age which, culturally speaking, ought to have been most prone of all to vulgar rusticity and upstart pretentiousness—the age of military government by the provincial samurai—was responsible for the type of plainness and unpreten-tiousness seen in the Japanese castle and the tea ceremony.

In ancient times, of course, the smallness of the nation compared with other ancient states such as Egypt or Babylon meant that the accumulation of wealth was also smaller. A more important differ-ence, however, was that from ancient times it was very rare for the authorities to make excessive demands for labor on the people. In-deed, the Nihon Shoki, which was compiled by the court, makes specific references to the people's dislike of large-scale undertakings.

The reason here was not a shortage of accumulated wealth or of labor, but of natural and social conditions in Japan, which by im-posing certain limitations on ways of life in Japan also determined the emotions and sensibility of the Japanese, so that all cultural manifestations came to fit in with them. Japan undoubtedly could have produced such massive buildings at the time if it had wanted to; its failure to do so was due less to economic limitations than to the typical modes of cultural expression of the Japanese. For in-stance, at the time of the building of a palace at Nagaoka in the reign of the Emperor Kammu, seven months were spent on the work by 314,000 peasants, but since it was still not completed, it was aban-doned and the palace of Heian built in the province of Yamato instead.

There is an almost ridiculous disparity between this kind of thing and what happened in other countries. The buildings of Egypt were the largest in the world. The stone palace of Karnak, which is said never to have been surpassed in scale, took an almost unbelievable seven hundred years to complete, whereas a mere seven months in Japan

was considered excessively long! The scale of the palace, too, was such that even now engineers are not sure how some things were achieved. Even the Pyramids, which are smaller, are said each to have employed 100,000 slaves—working in the three months when the Nile floods made other work impossible—for a full twenty years. The total number of man-days involved was some 18 million, a figure beside which the labor used on Japanese palaces is quite insignificant. All this was done to satisfy a taste for material display and for the imposing.

This kind of thing is unknown among the Japanese, nor do they have any desire to do it. Their ways of life make such a desire impossible. This overbearing type of taste does not inspire the average Japanese with respect nor awe, but appalls him. The Japanese look to a building, not to oppress them with its size, but to display a delicacy of sensibility. They lavish this sensibility on extremely small details. Architectural beauty is found in the way a wooden pillar is shaved, in the proportions of a room, in simple but delicate lines, and in other small things which are hardly taken into account at all in the West.

This same trait marks the Japanese character in every aspect, and is very clearly apparent in all cultural, as well as political, manifestations. It is, in fact, a characteristic of the national way of life.

It is interesting here to consider a country such as England which, though lying a little further north than Japan, resembles it in many respects. The climate is a little colder, but the scale is small. The national sensibility, too, is similar, and lacks the massive, continental aspects of, say, Egypt. Yet English architecture is nevertheless different from that of Japan. In respect of delicacy of sensibility, Japanese and English buildings are obviously different. A good example is the Henry VII chapel at Westminster, with its celebrated fan vaulting, in which stone is carved to produce an effect of lightness and delicacy which suggests some entirely different material. The labor involved is certainly great, but no Japanese could ever

produce such a work. Stone must be used so as to look like stone. No Japanese would want to use stone in a building so that it looked like the inside of a Japanese umbrella, or a spider's web. Such methods involve an enormous waste of labor. In China, too, great ingenuity is lavished on stone work; the Altar of Heaven in Peking, for example, has a balustrade of marble or some such stone with very elaborate carving. It is a characteristic of the Japanese that they would never do such a thing.

The cultural sensibility of the Japanese rejects such fruitless expense of labor in favor of the delicacy that comes from long training. Japan is different from China or the West even in the way it makes a single wooden pillar, which in Japan will reveal a use of the plane which took dozens of years to perfect. This kind of thing is not possible merely by increasing the amount of labor. With training, it is possible to produce with a single plane a surface like a mirror. The Japanese look for a delicacy of sensibility, expressed via technique, which is lacking in the West. A particularly glaring example of the difference is to be found in Kensington Palace, designed by the same Christopher Wren as was responsible for St. Paul's Cathedral. Here the lower part of the building has real pillars, the upper part painted pillars. Part of a real building, in short, is treated as though it were a piece of scenery on a movie set. Similarly, the materials used in the great buildings of China are extraordinarily rough-and-ready. Many of them are crudely painted in primary colors on a way that would be considered fit only for toys in Japan. Japanese Buddhist temples, being derived from those of China, are often colored, but a great deal of trouble is taken over where and how the lacquer is applied.

Another example is seen in warrior's clothing. Japanese military dress paid a great deal of attention to small details almost invisible to the casual observer. Again, women in the West tend to choose primary colors and to pay great attention to overall effect, whereas the Japanese woman pays incomparably more attention to details. The effect achieved, moreover, avoids overstimulating effects, bring-

ing subdued, natural colors to the outside and relegating bright colors, of the kind Westerners wear on the outside, to underwear which is hidden from view. Very often, great delicacy is shown in small details; it is considered a disgrace, for example, for a single stitch to be visible on the exterior of a kimono.

This same tendency is apparent in every aspect of culture, and, along with the other, related characteristics already discussed, clearly reveals the basic nature of Japanese civilization as a whole. Far from hindering Japan's national development, this basic nature, I believe, can, on the contrary, serve as a form of self-discipline preventing civilization from developing in a wild, uncontrolled fashion.

VIII JAPANESE CULTURE AND NATURE

An important characteristic of Japanese culture is its respect for nature and for actuality. Simplicity and austerity are features of that culture in all its forms, a fact which is nowhere more apparent than in architecture. Although in their temple architecture the Japanese erected large numbers of massive buildings in the Chinese style—buildings, moreover, with an elaboration of detail reminiscent of the cathedrals of medieval Europe—yet in the buildings which formed the strongholds of their daily lives, be they ordinary dwellings, palaces or castles, they have since ancient times resolutely rejected the foreign styles adopted in official public buildings in favor of a purely Japanese style. There is a marked contrast here with the dwellings of kings, aristocrats and local lords in China, India, and Europe, which displayed a grandeur unsurpassed by any public edifice.

This preference of the Japanese is very stubborn, and frequently shows a fine disregard for practical convenience. The castles of medieval times—which were, after all, buildings erected for military purposes—managed to suppress this deeprooted preference for wood to the extent of substituting clay walls for wooden walls on the exterior, but even this was done in a half-hearted fashion. Without exception, castles inside had the ordinary upper-class residential quarters made of wood. The outside was coated with plaster to prevent the enemy's setting fire to the structure, but concealed inside a wooden house of a kind very susceptible to fire—a peculiarly

pointless inconsistency from a military point of view. Yet tastes ingrained from ancient times were too strong to allow the Japanese to remedy this inconsistency.

One reason for the simplicity and austerity of the imperial palace in Japan was, of course, that there was no need to make the ruler's dwelling into a castle as in other countries. Even so, one might have expected just a little more visible splendor, if only as a symbol of the authority of the imperial family. In practice, though, there were only a very few cases of attempts to rival China by building palaces of any size in ancient times, and even here the project was abandoned in most cases because of the burden on the common people. The reason, of course, was that unlike in China, India, and Europe, even the ancient imperial system in Japan had no large supply of slave labor at its command. Because of such circumstances, simplicity and austerity automatically came to characterize the national culture, even where the architecture of the imperial palace itself was concerned. The *shinden-zukuri* style of architecture, which represents perhaps the most highly developed form reached by the aristocratic dwelling in ancient times, is an austere structure open to the elements and utterly unlike the residences of the aristocracy of China, India, or Europe.

For all the freedom with which the Japanese took over elements from foreign civilization and foreign taste, in their own, personal ways of life the Japanese of ancient times insisted on preserving and creating anew things of their own as well. And in doing this they were guided from first to last by a profound respect for nature and reality. Thus the predominance of plain, unpainted wood in architecture, and the "open" style which incorporated the garden and surrounding nature into the whole architectural design, are expressions of a desire to be with nature and not to tamper with its actualities.

It is all the odder, then, that the Japanese should have proved so

inadequate in their intellectual appreciation of the realities of nature.

Japanese literature has never shown the direct appreciation of nature that is apparent in the literature of China or the West. Even in contemporary literature, very few writers excel in natural descriptions. In the *waka*, that most characteristic form of Japanese literature, natural description has been a weak point ever since the time of the *Manyōshū*. In respect of nature as everything else, the Japanese sensibility is lyrical. Thus the celebrated scenery of Yoshino-yama, so beloved of the aristocrats at the Yamato court in ancient times, provided a suitable setting for lyrical outpourings, but was never appreciated directly for its own sake. The poetic references to Yoshino-yama in the *Manyōshū* are, one and all, intellectualized accounts. Even the celebrated verses on Mount Fuji written by Yamabe no Akahito are merely an intellectual account of what has been said about the mountain since ancient times: "I went out from Tago Bay and lo! Mount Fuji's lofty peak was mantled with snow." The reply, "Let us talk of it, sing its praises, for generations to come," is a perfect illustration of the unsophistication of the Japanese approach to nature; the attempt at realism is interesting, but even here the reality described is not a seen reality but a reminder of the saying that "the poet sees the beauty spot without stirring from his chamber."

It is true, of course, that Japanese garden design has nowadays become world-famous for its imitations of nature, and that experts come from all over the world to see it, but even here the view of nature tends to be intellectualized. Compared with Western "landscape gardening," of course, it can be said to be more delicate, profound, and perhaps civilized in its apprehension of nature, but the tendency nevertheless is to transmute nature into forms, and to view its separate parts without any comprehensive attempt to appreciate nature as a whole. It is the same love of detail as is seen in the miniature tree and the miniature landscape on a tray. The fond-

ness of the Japanese for creating in one garden dozens of "scenic spots" is another witness to their failure really to appreciate the larger panoramas of nature.

The Japanese approach to nature, thus, is a literal case of not seeing the wood for the trees. Their feeling for woods and forests is, in fact, extremely poor; they have never quite shaken off primitive man's fear of the forest, and its profound mysteries for them have no more than a superficially mysterious or magical significance. Even at this simple level, one might have expected the forest to inspire a certain amount of poetry or prose, but in practice it is absent from Japanese poetry, novels, and drama alike, and the Japanese equivalents of Robin Hood, William Tell, and Siegfried lack their true setting. The only major figures who come from the forests are for the most part bad men, who are not even said to come from the "forests," but from the "hills." The reason, of course, is the persistence of the primitive fear of the forest just mentioned.

Primitive man himself, however, lived originally in the forest. Man did not come to dread the forest until he had emerged from it and begun to live by agriculture rather than by hunting. The Japanese fear of the forest, thus, is a sign that from early antiquity they had advanced from the stage of agriculture, and that in the age of the myths Japanese civilization had already reached a fairly high level. Seen in this light, the fear of the forest has a respectable history; yet it remains true that when man progresses one stage further and begins to live in towns, he normally "returns to nature," and conceives a new affection for the forest. It is this that characterizes the feeling for the forest of man at his most civilized.

The Japanese, however, continued to shun the forest even after they had entered the age of the cities. Though continuing to use wood exclusively for their architecture and for all kinds of articles of everyday use, exhibiting an appreciation of the medium more refined than that of any other people, they proved incapable, oddly enough, of enjoying the surroundings which had produced it.

This flaw in the Japanese feeling for nature led to a deplorable tendency for the taste of the Japanese to deny nature once their civilization had reached its most advanced stage. It is a general rule that a race deficient in its appreciation of nature is necessarily deficient in cultural creativity also, since cultural forms are, ultimately, idealized re-creations of "nature," reproductions of "nature" in terms of human sensibility. Thus the failure of the presentday Japanese to appreciate nature means that modern Japanese culture cannot be truly creative.

It is only to be expected that Japanese towns today should be no more than imitations of their Western counterparts. There is nothing wrong in imitation of the West as such, but the Japanese have forgotten to imitate one of the most vital aspects of all—the superior feeling of the West for nature.

Where does the heart of a civilized city lie? It lies, it is said, in the spaces which serve to purify, physically and spiritually, the city atmosphere befouled by the unnaturalness of urban living. The Japanese are utterly unaware of how to provide such a heart—in other words, how to "naturalize" the spaces of their cities. Westerners always provide it in the form of the wooded parks which are a feature of all large cities in the West. Hyde Park in London, the Tiergarten in Berlin, the Bois de Boulogne in Paris—in all of them woods of living trees serve as the "heart" of the city, feeding fresh air to the hearts and minds of the city-dwellers. The Japanese neglect this. Tokyo, fortunately, has the Imperial Palace grounds which, though not open to the public, serve as the heart of the city, but when all is said and done, they are a legacy of the Tokugawa period, totally unrelated in their origins to the outlook of the modern Japanese.

As a result, the inhabitants have to take their pleasures in districts such as the Ginza or Shinjuku, in an atmosphere polluted in every sense of the word. Nor are these amusement areas in any sense a product of typically Japanese cultural modes, but are "colonial"

amusement districts, transplantations of all that is most vulgar in the third-rate quarters of Western cities. Few phenomena could display Japan in such a backward light as these.

Here again, the blame must be attributed to the failure of the Japanese to appreciate nature as a whole. A partiality for miniature trees or tray landscapes can never provide a basis for a popular, national awareness, both intellectual and emotional, of the delights of nature. The Japanese in their town planning may know how to make, here and there, small parks reminiscent of tray landscapes, but they do not know how to create wooded parks that bring to mind nature in all its grandeur. For all the deficiencies of the Japanese in this respect, the inhabitants of medieval Edo, much as is done in the cities of the West, at least created here and there in the very center of the city areas known as *sannai* which imitated natural woods, but even this degree of civilization in the approach to nature is lacking in the Japanese of today.

The tendency of the Japanese to view nature in its parts rather than as a whole is fully apparent in the arrangement of Japanese cities. The different quarters of a city ought to have their own atmospheres that depend on the daily activities of their inhabitants. Even today, indeed, terms such as "industrial district" and "commercial district" are still in use. Yet depending on whether or not each district is the product of a particular cultural outlook, it can become either something with a definite atmosphere of its own or a hopeless jumble.

Japanese cities today have no atmosphere; they show none of the cultural characteristics, symbolizing the ways of life of their citizens, that were apparent in the towns of the middle ages. There are distinctions between residential districts and downtown districts, but the two types of district in themselves display none of the outward forms that should precisely symbolize the kinds of life lived in them. Wherever one goes, the confusion of the newly built-up district rules the day.

Of course, it can hardly be expected that merchant houses and private mansions should still exhibit common, unifying features now that the guild-type restrictions of the middle ages no longer apply, yet if only the modern freedom were tempered by certain standards of civic sensibility, a symbolic unity would emerge in the natural course of events. In a town which preserves its ancient traditions, an indefinable classical atmosphere hovers about the place in spite of modern developments. Yet, when the modernization of commerce led to the destruction of the old wholesalers' quarters in Japanese towns, they failed completely to establish any definite new atmosphere, based on a more modern civic sensibility, to take its place, and the result was the creation of a town that looked as though a box of toys had been upset, the product of the individual whims of a lot of feebly Western-style architects.

The Ginza district, for example, is the spilt box of toys at its most extravagant. Considered individually, there are buildings to match those found in the cities of the West, but as a whole they are merely lined up as at an exhibition, proud in their individuality, without a care for where they are; each building stands isolated, its eyes closed to its surroundings. Thus no overall atmosphere can emerge, and chaos reigns. The gentleman in tails and the rouged-cheeked jester, Cleopatra and the crudely made-up country wench, sit side by side.

This type of chaos shares common origins with the inability of the Japanese to appreciate nature as a whole rather than as a number of parts.

IX   THE RENAISSANCE IN JAPAN

I

It would be difficult to find a period in Japanese history exactly corresponding to the Renaissance in Europe, but the nearest thing to it can perhaps be found in the literary revival of the mid-Tokugawa period. It was this period that first saw the emergence of cultural forms of an entirely different type from those of the aristocratic and warrior ages, and along with them one can detect the emergence of something resembling the humanism of Renaissance Europe. However, this Japanese "renaissance" did not stem from the same historical factors as led to its European counterpart, and its "humanism" was inevitably even vaguer than the imprecisely defined humanism of the West.

It is true, of course, that in medieval Japan as in Europe the church (in Japan's case the Buddhist temples) had a monopoly of learning and education, since the feudal ruling class as such completely lacked the ability to lead the country in this respect. However, the temples also played a leading part in new literary and artistic developments of considerable distinction, so that the literary and artistic revival of the Tokugawa period must be considered, not as entirely divorced from the medieval period, but as differing from it qualitatively insofar as it was a reflection of the development of the merchant society.

The process was, as elsewhere, a discovery of man—man as distinct from the religion of the temples and the orthodox morality. This was true of specific modes of expression just as it was of general trends in ideas. And where it took a full two centuries in Europe

from the start of the Renaissance to the birth of Shakespeare, in Japan it was as if Boccaccio, Shakespeare and Leonardo da Vinci had all appeared together in a jumble, as if the *litterae humaniores* of Europe (in Japan, the revival of classical learning from Keichū on) had rubbed shoulders with the modern European popular verse (in Japan the *haiku* and *senryū* from Teitoku on) and the modern novel (in Japan, the popular romances of the Tokugawa era).

The historical transition from a feudal to a bourgeois society of the kind which lay behind the European Renaissance, together with the humanism which was its expression, was making steady progress in Japan at this period. Japan lagged behind Europe, of course, in both range and intensity of international exchanges, but the process was essentially the same. The dependence of the Japanese economy on foreign trade from Ashikaga times on is witnessed by the attempt of the Ashikaga Shogunate to monopolize trade with the continent with its "Tenryū-ji ships." It was the development of the towns along the coasts of Kyūshū, central Honshū, the Osaka area, and northern Honshū as a result of the foreign trade which they conducted either openly or in secret that led the Japanese economy thereafter to place increasing emphasis on mercantilism. It seems likely that the *wakō*—which were no more nor less than trading vessels, whether armed or unarmed—were far more numerous than is suggested by written records alone. It was thanks to them that Japan, toward the end of the Sengoku period, enjoyed a period of unparalleled cultural brilliance.

Despite the policy of seclusion adopted by the Tokugawa Shogunate out of fear of aggression in the guise of foreign religions, foreign exchanges—whether via Chinese and Dutch merchants or not—did not come to a halt. The government's rash move in cutting down foreign trade by isolating the country, coming at a time when the agricultural economy no longer had the strength to support the finances of the feudal state, was to hasten the collapse of that state

rather than to cut short the rise of a bourgeois society. At this period, cultural forms in Japan had already embarked on a process of transition from the feudal to the bourgeois, and the process was quite firmly established. In short, many of the conditions that went to create the age of humanism in Europe were also present in Japan at this period.

Yet despite these similarities, the question remains of whether there was anything in Japan corresponding to the authority of the Christian church, without which it seems unlikely that humanism would ever have arisen in Europe. Without something in Japan to correspond in power and scope to the authority of Rome—and of course there was nothing—what was there for the humanistic trend to oppose itself to?

2

As we have already seen, medieval Japan resembled Europe in that the church held a monopoly of all culture and learning at the time. However, the cultural monopoly enjoyed by the Buddhist temples in Japan at this period was a natural outcome of the collapse of the aristocratic culture of ancient times, as a result of which the role it had hitherto fulfilled naturally passed to the temples; it was not, as in the case of the Roman Catholic church, the result of deliberate moves made by the organized authority of the church. It was a privilege maintained thanks to the cultural role of the priesthood rather than the religious and political authority of a European-style Church. To put it in a different way, the priesthood played the part of an intellectual class in medieval—i.e., samurai—society. The temples of medieval Japan, far from developing in the European fashion toward the exercise of absolute rule over the warrior state, actually made the priesthood one of the most important props of that state.

In Japan, the supremacy of the church, even over the small feudal domains of the day, was never established; instead of exercising authority over the state, it served it in a cultural capacity.

This does not imply, of course, that the temples developed in an exclusively cultural role. Indeed, their estates were large enough to constitute small feudal entities in much the same way as the powerful local clans, and they accumulated wealth and military strength which rivalled that of the samurai state. As a result, the temples formed a kind of covert opponent of that state, and they found themselves dispensing education, nor merely in the peaceful arts, but in the martial arts as well. The popular tale of how Yoshitsune, brought up at Kurama Temple, became sufficiently skillful with the sword to overcome the mighty Benkei, may be a figment of the popular imagination, yet it bears witness to the fact that the temples during the age of samurai rule fulfilled a far-ranging educational function among the local clans—a function extending to the political and military, and not merely the cultural—spheres.

This fact was less an outcome of the social role of the temples as such than of the special privileges which they enjoyed as monasteries, which put them beyond the reach of governmental and other secular authority and made of them a haven for the steady stream of vanquished warriors produced by the shifting fortunes of the local clans during the warrior age. Indeed, not only the defeated, the despairing, and the crossed in love, but the successful also, their worldly fame and achievements secure, shaved their pates and used the priestly privilege to give them a vantage-point from which to survey the world at leisure. This custom continued until the end of the Tokugawa period, and was taken advantage of not only by the warrior class but also by the aristocrats and merchants who ranked above and below that class respectively. However, the temples which gave shelter to these ''escapists'' who never immersed themselves totally in the religious life, these men whom Priest Saigyō called ''world-forsakers who could not forsake the world,'' inevitably ended up as

60

monasteries for—or, rather, the headquarters of—scholars and military men in the purely secular sense, particularly at the beginning of the period of samurai rule. In fact, the part played by the priesthood as the sole intellectual class of the warrior state following the establishment of the Kamakura Shogunate was much the same as that played by naturalized Chinese and Koreans in the preceding Nara and Heian periods. Moreover, since there was the world of difference between the ignorant samurai and the cultivated aristocrats of the preceding periods, the functions of the priesthood were doubtless still more comprehensive and unfettered than those of the immigrant scholars. Yet for all this, the role of the priests remained an intellectual one, and they never acquired ecclesiastical authority as such.

3

It seems likely that this predominantly cultural and intellectual—as opposed to ecclesiastical—authority of the priesthood in medieval Japan was an outcome of the peculiar forms assumed by religious belief in this country. The normal course of events in almost all countries before medieval times was that indigenous national beliefs were gradually replaced by a broader, supra-national faith. In the process, a certain number of the characteristics of the former were carried over into and fused with the latter, so that in the end one single religion was left, as before, with undisputed supremacy. In the civilized countries of today, all kinds of religions exist side by side, but such freedom of belief was quite impossible up to medieval times, and the world religions of the middle ages held exclusive sway in much the same way as the national religions had done before them. Thus the rise in the West of a world religion—Christianity—led eventually to the establishment of the Christian faith and its controlling organ, the Church, as a single, absolute, supranational authority. The Christian church, as a world religion, exercised the

same kind of unified control as the national religions of ancient times, and the success of Rome in establishing its absolute, supranational rule over the world was no different from the way in which the central churches of the ancient national faiths had exercised authority over their respective nations.

In medieval Japan, the conditions necessary for such a development did not exist. Even in the ancient period, before the feudal partitioning of the country, Japanese religion resembled that of the civilized countries of today in having lost its single, unified character. Contact between the national religion of ancient times and a new world religion did not lead, as in the West, to a wholesale switch from the former to the latter, but to a coexistence of the two similar to that found in those modern states which preserve freedom of belief. However, whereas in the modern state such coexistence means that the people are divided among two or more different religions, each with their different beliefs, in Japan the different religions held joint sway. The new world religion was laid on top of the indigenous faith, which the Japanese continued to profess as before. Nor, in Japan, was it merely that any other world religion could take its place alongside the indigenous faith, since other, not specifically religious, beliefs as well could coexist amicably with them. This peculiarity is seen at its most characteristic in the Middle Ages, when a blend of Shintō, Confucianism, and Buddhism came to constitute a far-reaching and powerful national system of belief.

The only exception to this general trend was Catholicism, which reached Japan around that time and which showed the same obstinate and characteristically Western rejection of all other faiths as it had elsewhere. However, it proved necessary for non-religious—political—reasons to prevent what must, in medieval times, have been the inevitable spread of the faith in Japan. Even had Catholicism not been suspect as a possible precursor of military and political aggression, its insistence on sole control to the exclusion of other faiths would, unless modified, have made it incompatible with the

traditional Japanese rejection of sole and absolute religious authority from abroad. It was only through a kind of fusion with Shintō—the *honchi suijaku* theory—that Buddhism had escaped being rejected, and one suspects that even medieval Catholicism, if allowed to exist in Japan a little longer, would eventually have shown a tendency to blend with the existing religions.

The reason why religion in ancient and medieval Japan should have presented features so unusual in the world of that time may perhaps be sought in the merging of faiths which resulted from the merging of peoples shown by anthropological studies to have occurred during the formation of the Japanese nation. Various processes of fusion and mixing seem to have been involved here, and the last of them—the mixing of the two great groups known as the Yamato race and the Izumo race—would necessarily seem to imply a fusing of the primitive religions of the two groups. For two races in ancient times to join together comparatively peacefully without some fusion between their religions would have been impossible from the outset.

It seems probable, thus, that already in prehistoric times the bases for a pluralized faith had been laid. For different faiths to exercise joint sway over a people is quite different from the existence of different faiths side by side, and quite a long preparatory period is certainly necessary before such a religious outlook can become possible. The psychological process involved in the switch from an indigenous faith to another at a higher cultural level is relatively simple, but to introduce the latter while still preserving the former requires some kind of conscious process of synthesis rather than a simple "switch." When Confucianism first came to Japan, the nature of this early Confucianism was such that a clash with the indigenous faith was unlikely, and it was possible for it to be taken over without trouble. The introduction of Buddhism, however, met with considerable difficulties. That it should have been decided to allow Buddhism, experimentally and conditionally, after submitting the question to what might almost be called "free discussion," is

enough to suggest the existence in Japan at the time of a relatively highly developed cultural consciousness. Such a highly developed consciousness could only be the result of some process of historical development, and it seems reasonable to suppose that this consisted in the process of blending of faiths which accompanied the peaceful fusion of races that began in prehistoric times.

Whatever the case, plurality of faith was a Japanese tradition from ancient times on. It was this that prevented the Buddhist temples from gaining sole sway over the country; the conditions necessary before ecclesiastical authority could become something absolute and transcending the state were simply not present.

4

The effect of these hidden factors was to restrict the temples in medieval Japan to a chiefly cultural and intellectual role, so that they were unable to exercise the absolute authority of the Church in the West.

62   The late Uemura Kankō, well known for his studies of the "Five Monasteries" literature which formed the central focus of Buddhist culture during the Ashikaga period, made some interesting observations in this connection. Comparing, in relation to culture, the position of the medieval monasteries of Europe and the temples of Japan, he says: "The culture of modern Europe represents mainly a revival which began around the sixteenth century, but its roots can be traced to studies of the arts and sciences of ancient Greece made by men of the Renaissance; the achievements of the medieval Christian monks were, from this point of view, more harmful than beneficial. The scholars of the Five Monasteries, on the other hand, continued even during Japan's "Dark Ages" to go back and forth busily between Japan and China. They brought back with them its civilization, which they themselves studied, championed, and instilled into

others, till eventually they were responsible for the flourishing of Confucian studies during the three hundred years of the Tokugawa period. . . . The monks of medieval Europe, on the other hand, as no one would be likely to dispute nowadays, were utterly different. In fact, the way they treated all learning as an accessory to theology—transformed it, rather, into theology—represented a departure from the Greeks' attitudes to study and only served to impair the independence of learning. In this respect, the scholars of the Five Monasteries were, if anything, closer to the humanism of the Renaissance period, and their achievement greater than that of the European monks.'' He also says, however, that ''the literature of the Five Monasteries consisted to a large extent of annotating and commenting, with very few original ideas,'' and in this respect too they resembled one aspect of European humanism.

It is clear, then, that the revival of Confucianism consequent on the introduction of Sung learning had the effect of giving cultural forms in Japan a still more eclectic nature. Nevertheless, the fact remains that in Japan this was still the formative period of medieval society, and as such represented a far earlier stage than that of humanism in Europe, where medieval society had already entered upon the process of dissolution. Its literature, for example, was deficient in humanistic tendencies in the modern sense; for such tendencies in literature of the day one must look, rather, to pseudo-archaic belles-lettres of the type of the *Hōjōki* and *Tsurezuregusa*. And this, as we shall see later, is related to the fact that Japanese literature of ancient times was essentially humanistic, so that any literary revival also had a humanistic flavor.

An important way in which Buddhist temples in Japan at the time differed from the Church in Europe was that since the Buddhist priests had no absolute authority and played a chiefly cultural role, they could take the place of the Confucian scholars of ancient times and carry out a Confucian revival. This was of course partly a reflection of developments in China, where the out-and-out rejection

of Buddhism of the T'ang period had given way in Sung times to a tendency to blend Confucianism and Buddhism. Still more, however, would it seem to have been due to the peculiarly Japanese way in which no single authority was ever allowed to hold absolute sway in the realms of faith and ideas.

The Confucianism revived by the priests of the Ashikaga period was no more than the intellectual culture of the ancient period—which derived from a fusion of Buddhism and Confucianism—refashioned so as to fit in with the modes of samurai rule. Probably the most conspicuous difference between this fusion in ancient times and in the medieval period was that in the former, more was made of the political morality of early Confucianism than of the religious goal of human salvation, whereas in the latter the religious awareness of the individual took precedence over the moral and political awareness of the ruler. In the time of the ancient aristocracy, both Buddhism and Confucianism found expression in the public or cultural sphere, but in the time of the medieval warrior their expression was more practical and personal. In other words, both Confucianism and Buddhism came in one sense to have a more direct bearing on the individual's life. The reason, doubtless, was that the life of the samurai class in the Middle Ages was far less stable and more subject to fluctuation than that of the aristocracy of olden times, so that there was a far stronger need for the religious in the life of the individual. As Tsuchiya Senkyō, author of *A History of Japanese Religion*, has most aptly put it, "Although the predominantly Buddhist religion of the Heian period was not lacking in grandiose aspects, its glory, even at its height, was only a matter of external appearances; true religious activity and the spread of great teachings among the Japanese people did not come until the non-aristocratic or popular religions of medieval times arose and overthrew the religion of the court and the priesthood."

In this medieval period, the fusion of Buddhism and Confucianism

ceased almost entirely to find expression in political, or in national and social terms. It was replaced on the one hand by Zen, the practical, down-to-earth faith of the warrior class, and, on the other, by the newly arisen popular faiths of the Shin and Nichiren sects, which replaced the superstition-laden faiths—typified by the Shugendō—of the previous age. Both the latter were well fitted, with their relatively simple doctrines, to the winning-over of the non-cultured masses. The only thing to correspond in any way to the "religion of the ruling class" of the Heian period was the Zen of the warrior class. All the rest were popular religions, with the result that the temples themselves gradually became divorced from the patronage of the aristocracy and warriors and began to exist as a power in their own right. Toward the end of the Heian period, the growth of the temple estates had made the great monasteries into feudal "states" in the same way as the powerful provincial clans, and armed struggles occurred between monastery and monastery. Now, in the Sengoku age, the temples of the newer sects accumulated military might in their turn on the basis of funds provided by the contributions of believers. This led to frequent military disputes of a typically feudal nature involving the temples. Particularly notorious here were the Ikkō risings of the Shin sect, and the behavior of the Nichiren sect. It was during this same period that the infiltration of Japan by Christianity began, and it seems likely—if the Shimabara rebellion of later years is anything to judge by—that if it had only received public recognition a little earlier it would have established itself as a feudal entity in no way inferior to Buddhism.

From the Kamakura period until the end of the Sengoku age, thus, the fusion of Shintō, Buddhism, and Confucianism depended chiefly on the initiative of the priests. Shintō, it is true, managed a certain degree of independent development from the time of Kitabatake Chikafusa on, but this tended toward forced interpretations of the classics in the Buddhist or Taoist manner, and lapsed into low-grade

63

64

65

66 mysticism of the type typified by the Yuiitsu Shintō of Urabe Kanetomo. As an institutional force it never succeeded in developing in any way comparable with Buddhism.

Since the power which the temples acquired in this period was, unlike its counterpart in medieval Europe, essentially an element within the feudal organization, it was possible later for Tokugawa Ieyasu to suppress it in the course of his unification of the country, and the temples were forced to return to their original organization. On top of this, the temples were also to lose their monopoly of learning.

5

It was the Tokugawa government which made the new Confucian learning nurtured by the Zen priests independent of the priesthood. The first step in the freeing of Confucian scholarship from depend-
67 ence on Buddhist scholarship occurred when Fukiwara Seika, orig- inally a priest of the Shōkoku-ji Temple, recommended that the Shogunate have his pupil Hayashi Razan build up an official system of Confucian studies on the basis of Sung learning. Within less than a century from this time—the century from the beginning of the Bunroku era, when Ieyasu summoned Seika, to the Genroku era, when the official Shogunate school, the Shoheikō, was established —Confucianism for the first time succeeded in establishing an authority independent of Buddhism.

Thus although the Buddhist church had failed to establish a supra- state authority—although, indeed, no European-style ecclesiastical authority had ever succeeded in establishing itself from ancient times right up to the Tokugawa period—in the latter period an authority approximating to this type did eventually assert itself.

Nevertheless, even this was not an authority standing above the state, but the official learning of the central feudal government.

Moreover, since it took an academic form totally divorced from anything truly religious, it never—even under feudal rule—went any further than a half-hearted and academic prohibition of other systems of learning; in this, it was poles apart from the intolerance of medieval Europe.

This official Confucianism of the Tokugawa period was the most organized official system of teaching that ever came into being in Japan, and the one that came nearest to practical enforcement of its authority. Yet by the time this happened, the feudal society which provided its background and its objective *raison d'etre* was already beginning to disintegrate. The merchant society which had gradually been taking shape since the Kamakura period underwent its own autonomous development during the Sengoku age. Everything—for example, the growth of the temples of the new popular sects to the point where their power outstripped that of the temples patronized by the warrior class, or the development of the tea ceremony, the essence of merchant culture, in the temples with lands in the commercial districts—bore witness to the growth of the merchant culture. The period centering around the Genroku era, which formed a kind of cultural peak in the Tokugawa period, was also the period when the economic bases of the military state were replaced by those of merchant society. It bore a strong resemblance to the period in Renaissance Europe when the wealth of the feudal states was replaced by that of the free cities.

Just as the first buddings of humanism in the Renaissance were a product of the culture of the cities, so the period around the Genroku era corresponded to the formative period for the culture of merchant society. In Japan at this point, however, the adversary against which humanism directed itself was the official Confucianism just discussed.

The nature of this humanism was most clearly shown in the *kogaku*—the revival of the study of the Japanese classics—which was initiated by men such as Keichū, Mabuchi, and Norinaga, but all the

newly arising forces in contemporary literature and art equally represented an escape from the hard shell of medieval samurai society. The novels and plays of Saikaku and Chikamatsu, for example, were obvious products of the modern age, quite distinct from the martial literature and "hermit" literature of the middle ages, while the ukiyo-e woodblock print and the Kabuki both developed under the patronage of the merchant class. Thus the new prototypes of culture all lay outside the sphere of the aristocracy and the samurai, and expressed the attitudes to life held by the bourgeoisie. In particular, the general availability of the polychrome print (nishiki-e, "brocade picture") consequent on the development of block printing, which paralleled the increased availability of books as a result of developments in ordinary printing techniques, gave birth to a unique type of art which showed how far the ways of life of the merchant society had replaced those of the aristocracy and the samurai at the center of the national life. In the fields of literature and painting too, the products of the aristocracy and warrior class came to have an antique flavor, while almost everything that was contemporary and alive was created in response to the demands of the merchant class.

The mainstream of culture in this period of change was "humanistic" insofar as it freed men and society from the intellectual sway of Buddhism and Confucianism and treated man and his environment as actualities in their own right. However, within the transition as it occurred in Japan there was a strong cultural continuity. For example, even though the Kabuki took the place of the Nō, in its modes of artistic expression it preserved to a certain extent the forms of the latter. At the same time, however, it moved away from the expression of essentially Buddhistic intellectual concepts, and toward the expression of human emotions. In every branch of learning and literature, the outward forms of the tradition were followed while departing further and further from it in content.

It was kogaku which showed most clearly this process of change. Among many manifestations of, inevitably, an interdeterminate hue,

kogaku set out unmistakably to define the intellectual modes of the new age, and in this sense the work of Motoori Norinaga can be called epochmaking.

6

One way in which Norinaga's *kogaku* was humanistic was that it began, not as something new and original, but as a return to the culture of ancient times. The special characteristics of this culture which he cites—in other words, the bases of his humanism—can be summarized as follows.

First, he distinguished the inevitability of history from intellectual ideas of purpose. As he saw it, history was not an expression of "how things should be," but of the *kokoroshiwaza* (spirit and deeds) of gods of the kind who appeared in Japan's mythological age. These gods were very varied in nature, some righteous and some unrighteous, some good and some evil. In times when evil gods were on the rampage the good gods were able to do nothing. However, when one viewed the whole history of the age of the gods as an expression of the will of the gods, it was clearly the *kokoroshiwaza* of the good gods that prevailed, so that this must represent absolute reality. However, since the power of the good gods against the arrogance of the bad gods was not always absolute, the *kokoroshiwaza* of the good gods could not make itself felt in the age of the bad gods. This was clear from the history of the Chinese mainland and of medieval Japan. Moreover, since in such cases efforts by human beings to remedy these phenomena only made matters worse, the only thing to do was to accept the vicissitudes of human affairs as they came.

This led some to say that Norinaga's philosophy was based on the idea of "nature" of Lao-tzu and Chung-tzu, but Norinaga denied this on two scores. First, he pointed out, his philosophy was based, not on any idea of "nature," but on the *kokoroshiwaza* of the gods.

145

Secondly, he was not concerned, in the fashion of Lao-tzu and Chung-tzu, with theories of how things ought to be. His philosophy treated history as the expression of the *kokoroshiwaza* of personified gods whose personalities were both righteous and wicked, with no teleological significance; thus their *kokoroshiwaza* were, ultimately, no different from the morally colorless Nature of the scientists. In this sense, Norinaga can be regarded as a kind of naturalist, and his ideas bore within them the seeds of post-humanist modern trends.

Secondly, Norinaga held views on man and morality similar to his views on history. He recognized no "sage," no perfect and ultimate being conforming to theoretical ideas of how things should be. Such a concept for him was no more than an ideal artificially created with the aim of imposing some unity on a state and society which had fallen into unnatural ways. Neither man nor society could ever be completely and spotlessly pure, and ideas of the "perfect" character were unrealistic. By their nature, says Norinaga, men "know what they have to know and do what they have to do." Since justice, courtesy, filial piety, loyalty, and the like are only natural to them, they will know what they have to know of these without being taught. To "try to instill these things into men to an unnatural degree," as do moral concepts specially devised to set right some unnatural state of affairs, is "coercion." Confucianism criticizes all opposition to such "coercion" as products of selfish "human desires," but so long as the morality designed to curb these is "coercion," then "are not human desires themselves the more natural order of things?"

Thirdly, Norinaga argues from this that true literature and art is that which gives expression to man in this sense, just as he is. He expressed this technically as "expressing *mono-no-aware.*" Whereas all literary critics before him had based their views on Buddhist or Confucian teleology, Norinaga insisted (with particular reference to the *Tale of Genji*) that ancient Japanese literature had in fact expressed nothing but this *mono-no-aware*. His *mono-no-aware* is, basically, the

natural expression of human emotions, but he points out, using Genji's words in the "Hotaru no Maki" chapter as an illustration, that the literary expression of these emotions has two aspects. The first moves the reader by giving him the feeling that the things described might actually have occurred—in other words, it is a realistic treatment. The other sets out to amaze by describing things which are extremely unlikely—in other words, a romantic or grotesque treatment.

Norinaga has his own view on the state, government, morality, education, and so on, all in line with these; and all are directed against Confucianism: in other words, they represent a humanistic trend running counter to the authority of the day.

That Norinaga should have been able to express his modern outlook in terms of a revival of ancient culture was only possible, of course, because of the existence, in the ancient prototypes of Japanese culture, of humanistic characteristics, and the absence in the Japanese classics of *a priori* reasoning and intellectualism of the kind found in the Chinese classics—its humanism, in other words—was due, as Norinaga suggests, to the fact that the state in Japan, unlike the state in continental countries, was founded not on a morality but on the idea of a family. The two views are admirably illustrated by the *Kojiki* and the *Shu-ching*, and the only reason Norinaga avoided the *Nihon Shoki* in favor of the *Kojiki* was that the former, though on the whole of course adopting the same outlook as the latter, showed in parts a "Chinese" intellectualism reminiscent of the Chinese work; it was not that he did not respect the *Nihon Shoki* as a history. The *Manyōshū* and the *Shih-ching* show a similar contrast, and 68 Mabuchi had already pointed out the intellectual interpretations of the *Shih-ching*.

The first compilation of histories and verse anthologies in Japan was motivated partly by a desire to emulate the culture of China, and also, probably, by the need, as exchanges with the continent developed, to foster a national consciousness. That the products of these

motivations should have been works so un-Chinese in outlook as the *Kojiki* and *Manyōshū* can only indicate the existence in Japan at the time of a culture of quite a high level, which made possible cultural expression in terms of the national character. The revivalism of Norinaga and his followers set up this ancient character and culture in opposition to the official teaching of medieval times.

7

The revival of classical learning was a powerful force which influenced contemporary ideas on the state, society, government, and morality alike, and played an intellectual role in preparing for the Meiji Restoration. However, as we have already seen, Japanese culture had always followed a conciliatory, eclectic course, and even around the Genroku era the traditional attitudes were observable in both learning and religion. Even Motoori Norinaga himself stuck to the Shin sect to which his family belonged, choosing his own posthumous Buddhist name and ordering that his funeral services should be conducted in the Buddhist style. This pragmatic trait in the Japanese seems to have been determined by the nation's unique history, in which from the time of the nation's first founding there was, as we have seen, none of the racial or religious strife common to other countries of both East and West. For this reason, the traditional Japanese outlook was itself, as a whole, humanistic. The indigenous and the foreign, the early and the late, one thing and another, were always obliged to come to terms, somehow, without falling at each other's throats. This being so, it was impossible that absolute authority should be given to any one system. One is reminded of the etiquette always observed between friend and foe among the samurai of medieval times, which is a sign of the way the Japanese character seeks to use the elements shared in common to reconcile every clash between interests.

148

In the age of the revival of classical learning, there was a parallel type of movement in Confucianism, typified by the Mito school, *69* while even in the official Chu Hsi school of Confucianists there were some, such as Kaibara Ekken, who taught the coexistence of Shintō- *70* ism and Confucianism. "It is the norm for ordinary human behavior," Ekken said of Shintōism. "It follows local customs and adapts itself to local needs. Its teachings are simple, neither over-complicated nor over-ingenious. . . . Its ceremonies are austere, neither showy nor elaborate; thus they never lose their sincerity. Its teachings appear to be commonplace, yet profundity resides within them. If only it is used to purify the heart and deeds and refurbish the morality of the people, then the land will be at peace, free from natural disasters and disturbances. . . . It is a way of thinking handed down by the gods and wise men of ancient Japan, and owes nothing to borrowings from abroad." This is almost literally identical with what Motoori Norinaga has to say. When one considers that a scholar of that very Confucianism against which the classical scholars took up arms—especially a man of the orthodox school such as Ekken— could say such things, one begins to wonder whether there was ever an official "system" of thought in Japan.

The reason was, however, that Shintō, the indigenous Japanese system, never developed as an official system, showing itself tolerant not only toward Confucianism but toward Buddhism as well, while those who took over the new religions, being themselves Japanese, were still more conciliatory in their outlook. In other countries, the normal course taken by religion in ancient and medieval times was for a newer and more advanced system to drive out the indigenous system and establish itself in a position of supremacy, but in Japan the old and the new blended together like two scenes on a twice-exposed photograph. This was not accomplished without a certain confusion, but the practical-minded Japanese accepted the confusion quite happily so long as it caused no practical difficulties. A case in point is the Zen priests of medieval Japan, who are more noted for

their contribution in spreading the new Confucianism—Sung learning—than in spreading their own religion. In the same way, Confucianism itself, even after it achieved its independence of Buddhism in the Tokugawa period, remained sufficiently practical in its outlook not to make any thoroughgoing attempt to disentangle the three religions of Shintōism, Confucianism, and Buddhism.

NOTES

1. *Mononobe*. A powerful family of ancient times whose members for many generations held important positions at court. Following the introduction of Buddhism in the sixth century, they opposed the new religion from abroad as an insult to the native gods. They clashed violently with the Soga family, who were their rivals at court and ardent champions of Buddhism, and were finally defeated by them in 587.

2. *Minamoto and Taira*. The two great warrior clans whose rise at the end of the Heian period brought about the eclipse of the effete Kyoto aristocracy. The Taira gained the ascendancy temporarily, and enjoyed a brief period of glory, but they themselves showed a debilitating love of luxury, and were overthrown in their turn by the Minamoto, who established a shogunate in Kamakura under Yoritomo.

3. *Okinagusa*. A collection of essays in many volumes, published originally in 1772. It assembles from a large number of different sources strange and interesting legends and tales ranging in time from antiquity to the Edo period.

4. *kataribe*. Professional court reciters of history and legends in ancient times.

5. *Nihon Shoki*. An official history of Japan compiled in 720. Written in Chinese, it covers the period from the age of the gods up to the Empress Jitō (645–702).

6. *Kojiki*. A compilation of Japanese myths and history made at the command of the Emperor Gemmei (662–721) on the basis of old oral traditions, and completed in 712.

7. *Motoori Norinaga* (1730–1801). A philologist and student of the Japanese classics. He is famous for his studies of works such as the *Kojiki, Genji Monogatari*, and the *Kokinshū*, and for his rejection of Confucianism and emphasis on the native Japanese tradition—an emphasis which was to have a considerable influence on later nationalistic ideas.

8. *Manyōshū*. The oldest and most celebrated anthology of purely Japanese verse, containing some 4,500 poems written by members of all classes of society over a period of four or five centuries ending in 760.

9. *Kitabatake Chikafusa* (1292–1354). A courtier in the service of the Emperor Godaigo during the period of the Northern and Southern courts. Well versed in ancient history, he wrote, among other works, the *Jinnō Shōtōki*, an account of the Japanese

emperors from the age of the gods which was designed in part to prove the legitimacy of the Southern Court.

10. *Eiga Monogatari*. A historical work in Japanese relating in chronological order a number of interesting episodes from a period of some two hundred years from the early twelfth century.

11. *Genroku era* (1688–1703). An era which has come to symbolize the extraordinary flowering of literature, drama, and art which occurred in the middle of the Edo period. It is particularly associated with the culture of the luxury-loving merchants of Edo and Osaka.

12. *Keichū* (1640–1701). A Buddhist priest who was also a poet and student of classical Japanese literature. He is noted for his advocacy of a revival of the classical Japanese tradition as typified by the *Manyōshū*.

13. *Kamo Mabuchi* (1697–1769). A poet and student of classical Japanese literature in the mid-Edo period, one of the leading champions of the classical revival and teacher of Motoori Norinaga.

14. *Shu-ching*. A Chinese work on political history and political morality, one of the basic classics of Confucianism; also known as *Shang-shu*.

15. *Ōkagami*. A historical work of unknown authorship possibly completed in the time of the Emperor Shirakawa (1053–1129) or later. It takes the form of a discourse between two old men, with critical interpellations by a young samurai who is standing by listening, and deals with episodes from the period corresponding to the heyday of the Fujiwara family.

16. *Mizukagami*. A historical work, in the same vein as the *Ōkagami*, relating in chronological order episodes from the period preceding that dealt with in the other work.

17. *Azuma Kagami*. A historical work, compiled at the command of the Kamakura shogunate and recording in a mixture of Chinese and Japanese the history of the Kamakura shogunate from 1180 to 1266.

18. *Dai Nihon-shi*. A massive history of Japan from the Emperor Jimmu to the Emperor Gokomatsu in the early fifteenth century. A special bureau was set up in 1657 to start compilation of the work, and it was finally completed in 1906. With its emphasis on the unbroken succession of the Imperial family, it helped in reviving ideas of loyalty to the Emperor in the period preceding the Meiji Restoration.

19. *Nihon Gaishi*. A history in Chinese by Rai Sanyō, published in 1829 and dealing with the great warrior families of Japan from the Taira and Minamoto to the Tokugawa.

NOTES

20. *Ashikagas.* The samurai family which provided the shoguns who ruled Japan during the Muromachi period, which is also known as the Ashikaga period.

21. *Minamoto no Sanetomo* (1192–1219). The third Kamakura shogun.

22. *Hōjō era.* The period of more than a century, beginning in the early thirteenth century, during which the Hōjō family wielded power as hereditary "regents" advising the Minamoto who theoretically ruled the country as shoguns.

23. *wakō.* A name originally given in China and Korea to the Japanese—many of them pirates from the Inland Sea and Northern Kyūshū—whose ships infested the coasts of the Korean peninsula and China.

24. *Sengoku age.* The age of almost continuous civil strife which began at the end of the fifteenth century and ended with the unification of the country by Toyotomi Hideyoshi at the end of the sixteenth century.

25. *Tenryū-ji ships.* Trading vessels which Ashikaga Tadayoshi, in consultation with the celebrated monk Musō Kokushi, sent to Yüan China in the middle of the fourteenth century to earn funds for the building of the Tenryū-ji, a temple on the outskirts of Kyoto.

26. *Okakura Tenshin* (1862–1913). Author of the well-known *Book of Tea.*

27. *Sen no Rikyū* (1520–1591). A celebrated master of the tea ceremony, the man who perfected the ceremony in the rustic, unpretentious form familiar today. He worked in the service of Oda Nobunaga and later of Toyotomi Hideyoshi, but incurred the wrath of the latter and was ordered to commit suicide.

28. *Toyotomi Hideyoshi* (1536–1598). The great general who in the late sixteenth century succeeded in unifying the nation and making himself its effective ruler. On his death, his son was still a child, and a further short period of strife was followed by the victory of the Tokugawa family and the establishment by Ieyasu of the Tokugawa shogunate.

29. *tea party.* In October, 1587, Toyotomi Hideyoshi held a great tea ceremony at Kitano in Kyoto to which everybody, from whatever class of society, was invited. The fete lasted ten days, and was accompanied by various entertainments.

30. *Tokugawa Ieyasu* (1542–1616). The first Tokugawa shogun, the man who made Edo the effective capital of the country, started a dynasty which gave strife-torn Japan unity and peace for over two-and-a-half centuries, and initiated the policy of seclusion which was to shut Japan off almost entirely from the rest of the world until the arrival of Perry in the mid-nineteenth century.

30. *Ashikaga Yoshimasa* (1435–1490). The eighth Ashikaga shogun, celebrated as a patron of the arts.

153

32. *Nochikagami*. A history of the Ashikaga shoguns compiled at the order of the Tokugawa shogunate and completed in 1853.

33. *shoin-style (shoin-zukuri)*. A style of residential architecture which developed in the Muromachi and Momoyama periods and continues to form the basis of Japanese domestic architecture today.

34. *sarugaku*. A popular entertainment of great antiquity which seems to have consisted largely of song and mime and to have been based on popular tales and legends, often with a considerable humorous element. The dramatic element is believed gradually to have increased until it came to form one of the bases of the Nō drama.

35. *onna kabuki*. A type of dramatic entertainment consisting chiefly of song and dance which was popular around the beginning of the seventeenth century. The ancestor of the modern Kabuki, it is traditionally said to have originated with a dancer called Izumo Okuni, but was banned before long as detrimental to public morals. Following this the women's place was taken by youths, but they too were banned, and the result was the modern type of Kabuki in which all the parts are played by adult men.

36. *Heike Monogatari*. The celebrated martial epic, believed to have been written sometime after 1220, though there are various versions and elaborations of the text, the most substantial of them being the *Gempei Seisuiki*. Written in a type of prose-poetry combining stylistic characteristics of both Chinese and Japanese, it brings an essentially Buddhist outlook to bear on the struggle between the Taira and Minamoto families.

37. *Taiheiki*. A martial romance believed to have been written in the late fourteenth century. It deals with the disturbances of the period of the Northern and Southern courts, a period of over fifty years beginning in 1336.

38. *jōruri*. A type of ballad accompanied at first by the *biwa* (Japanese lute) or by tapping with a fan and later by samisen.

39. *kōdan*. Tales of a widely varying nature—martial, political, domestic, etc.— recounted by professional story-tellers.

40. *rakugo*. Humorous monologues by professional raconteurs, most of them anecdotes marked by a racy, plebeian sense of comedy and considerable powers of characterization.

41. *Ihara Saikaku* (1642–1693). A celebrated novelist and poet of the Edo period who wrote—in a style skillfully combining both traditional, literary and more popular, contemporary elements—a large number of works depicting the manners of the society of his time, from the rigid outlook of old-style samurai to the frivolous, luxury-loving and sensual lives of the merchant class in the large towns.

NOTES

42. *Genji Monogatari*. The *Tale of Genji*, the world-famous novel written at the beginning of the eleventh century by Murasaki Shikibu, a lady-in-waiting at court. It depicts court life in the Heian period via its account of the life and loves of its hero Hikaru Genji and his son Kaoru.

43. *Matsunaga Teitoku* (1571–1673). A celebrated *haiku* and *waka* poet of the Edo period, who first established many of the characteristic conventions of the *haiku* form.

44. *Gomizunoo* (1596–1680). Also known as Gominoo.

45. "Leaping . . ." The original contains an untranslatable play on words; the point here is that the poem's theme is homely, and that it uses a very popular and "un-literary" phraseology.

46. *Matsuo Bashō* (1644–1694). The most celebrated master of the *haiku*, who rid the form of the tendency to be merely clever and gave it a new spiritual profundity. Besides his verse, he is known for his poetic travel journals, of which *Oku no Hosomichi* is the most famous.

47. *kyōku, senryū, jiguchi*. Various forms of humorous or punning verse.

48. *Shōtoku Taishi* (574–622). A son of the Emperor Yōmei, who as Crown Prince under the Empress Suiko was virtual ruler of the country. An ardent champion of Buddhism and himself a scholar of some distinction, he is noted for having founded many temples in various parts of the country and, still more, for having applied the enlightened ethics of Buddhism—as embodied in his so-called "Constitution"—to the task of governing the country.

49. *Yoshida Kenkō* (1282–1350). A poet and essayist of the Kamakura period, especially noted for his *Tsurezure-gusa*, a collection of essays written in retirement as a monk.

50. *Kamo Chōmei* (1153–1216). A poet and writer of the Kamakura period, who in later life retired to a small rustic cottage where he wrote his celebrated *Hōjōki*, a discursive disquisition, heavily colored with Buddhistic ideas, on his own career and the impermanence of all worldly things.

51. *Tsubouchi Shōyō* (1859–1935). A novelist, dramatist, and critic also famous for his translations of Shakespeare.

52. *Futabatei Shimei* (1864–1909). A Meiji-period novelist noted for his new style, which made use of the colloquial language, and for his realism and psychological insight.

53. *Mori Ōgai* (1862–1922). A novelist, dramatist, critic, and army physician who in addition to his own creative work did much to introduce European, especially German, literature to post-Meiji Japan.

54. *Hōryū-ji Temple*. The oldest surviving Buddhist temple in Japan, containing the oldest wooden buildings in the world. Founded by Shōtoku Taishi and located close to the modern city of Nara, it is noted for the large number of ancient buildings and art treasures from various periods in its possession.

55. *shinden-zukuri*. The style of residential architecture favored by the aristocracy from the Nara period on. It consisted basically of a main building flanked by two sub-sidiary structures to which it was joined by galleries and from which further galleries extended at right angles to end in pavilions, with other subsidiary structures, a lake, etc., completing the whole plan. It was characterized by its extreme openness to the exterior and by the lack of separate rooms inside.

56. *"Those who stress . . ."* The reader should bear in mind the period at which the work was written.

57. *Tsurezure-gusa, Hōjōki*. See Notes 49 and 50 on Yoshida Kenkō and Kamo Chōmei.

58. *"both a Kiyomori and a Shigemori"*. Taira no Kiyomori was the general who in the late Heian period defeated the Taira's rivals, the Minamoto, and launched his family on its brief period of glory, during which, by political maneuverings and intermarriage with the imperial family, it became the most powerful force in the nation. His son Shigemori was noted for a caution and moderation which contrasted strongly with his father's forcefulness and impetuousness.

59. *Kogo Shūi*. A record in Chinese of the history of the Imbe family, which was for many years one of the families in charge of Shintō ritual at court. Compiled in 807 by Imbe no Hironari and presented to the Emperor, it contains a number of historical accounts omitted by the *Kojiki* and *Nihon Shoki*.

60. *Saigyō* (1118-1190). A poet-priest of the late Heian period. A samurai in the service of the ex-Emperor Toba, he took holy vows at the age of twenty-three, and spent the rest of his life traveling around the country as an itinerant priest.

61. *honji suijaku*. The theory of the essential identity of the native gods of Shintō and the various Buddhas and Bodhisattvas of Buddhism, the former being temporary manifestations of the latter designed to help the masses attain salvation.

62. *"Five Monasteries" literature*. The verse and prose written in Chinese by monks of the great Zen monasteries of Kamakura and Kyoto during the Kamakura and Muromachi periods.

63. *Shugendō*. A religious body deriving principally from the Esoteric Buddhism of the Shingon and Tendai sects. It flourished particularly during the Heian and early Kamakura periods, though it has survived right up to the present day. It is characterized by its love of rituals, spells, and ascetic practices, and by a kind of mountain worship.

64. *Ikkō risings*. Peasant risings by fanatical devotees of the Shin sect (the Amidist sect founded by Shinran), in league with the priests and minor lords. The risings were chiefly aimed at spreading the sect's beliefs and shaking off the feudal authority of the daimyos.

65. *Shimabara rebellion*. A rebellion of Japanese Christians which took place in 1637 near Nagasaki, in Kyūshū, in opposition to religious and, possibly, economic persecution. It was quelled with considerable difficulty, and large numbers of Christians were killed. It marked the final disappearance of Christianity from Tokugawa Japan, at least on the surface, and doubtless encouraged the government in its exclusionist policy.

66. *Yuiitsu Shintō*. A sect of Shintō begun by Urabe (or Yoshida) Kanetomo (1435–1511), who called for a return to "pure" Shintō, to the "way of the gods" untainted by any elements of Confucianism. However, his system was, in fact, highly eclectic.

67. *Fujiwara Seika* (1561–1619). A Confucian scholar of the early Edo period. He was a Buddhist priest, but took up the study of the neo-Confucianism of Chu Hsi, and eventually his fame as a Confucian scholar won the notice of Tokugawa Ieyasu, who summoned him to give his views on the shogunate's official system of learning. It was his pupil Hayashi Razan (1583–1657) who became the chief exponent of neo-Confucianist ideas and official adviser on Confucianism to the shogunate.

68. *Shih-ching*. The "Book of Odes," one of the basic classics of Confucianism.

69. *Mito school*. A school of historians which arose in the second half of the seventeenth century. It combined Confucianism with studies of Japanese literature and religion, which contributed considerably to the revivalist trend of later years.

70. *Kaibara Ekken* (1630–1714).

MEJ   6625

THE JAPANESE CHARACTER
日 本 的 性 格

昭和41年3月31日 発 行

著作権所有　　文 部 省
　　　　　　　東京都千代田区霞ヶ関 3 - 4

発 行 者　　講談社インターナショナル株式会社
　　　　　　　東京都文京区音羽町 3-19
　　　　　　　代表取締役　服 部 敏 幸

印 刷 者　　ゼネラル印刷株式会社
　　　　　　　横浜市中区扇町 3-108
　　　　　　　専務取締役　森　　菊 雄

発 行 所　　講談社インターナショナル株式会社

　　　　　　　　　　　　　　定 価　￥1,260